TADATOSHI FUJIMAKI

Whenever I go out to eat, I can't bear to order the same dish as anyone else in my party. No matter how much I want it, I'll always just change my order. I know it's pointless, but this is a rule I can never break.

—2010

Tadatoshi Fujimaki was born on June 9, 1982, in Tokyo. He made his debut in 2007 in *Akamaru Jump* with *Kuroko's Basketball*, which was later serialized in *Weekly Shonen Jump*. *Kuroko's Basketball* quickly gained popularity and became an anime in Japan in 2012.

Kuroko's BASKETBALL

5 & 6

SHONEN JUMP Manga Edition
BY TADATOSHI FUJIMAKI

Translation/Caleb Cook
Touch-Up Art & Lettering/Mark McMurray
Design/Sam Elzway
Editor/John Bae

KUROKO NO BASUKE © 2008 by Tadatoshi Fujimaki
All rights reserved.
First published in Japan in 2008 by SHUEISHA Inc., Tokyo.
English translation rights arranged by SHUEISHA Inc.

The stories, characters and incidents mentioned in this publication are entirely fictional.

No portion of this book may be reproduced or transmitted in any form or by any means without written permission from the copyright holders.

Printed in the U.S.A.

Published by VIZ Media, LLC
P.O. Box 77010
San Francisco, CA 94107

10 9 8 7 6 5 4 3 2 1
First printing, December 2016

www.viz.com

SHONEN JUMP MANGA

I KNEW IT 5

TADATOSHI FUJIMAKI

Kuroko's BASKETBALL

CHARACTERS

TAIGA KAGAMI

A first-year on Seirin High's basketball team. Though he's rough around the edges, he's a gifted player with a lot of potential. His goal is to beat the Miracle Generation.

TETSUYA KUROKO

A first-year on Seirin High's basketball team. Gifted with a natural lack of presence, he utilizes misdirection on the court to make nearly invisible passes.

KUROKO'S BASKETBALL

One of the Miracle Generation. Any basketball move he sees, he can mimic in an instant.

A second-year on Seirin High's basketball team. As captain, he led his team to the Finals League last year despite only playing first-year players.

A second-year who's the coach of Seirin High's basketball team.

A first-year on Shutoku High's basketball team. He carts Midorima around in a rickshaw. His abilities are unclear at this point.

The top shooter of the Miracle Generation. He plans everything according to his horoscope.

A third-year on Shutoku High's basketball team. As captain, he helped crush Seirin High in last year's Finals League.

Teiko Middle School is an elite championship school whose basketball team once fielded five prodigies collectively known as "the Miracle Generation." But supporting those five was a phantom sixth man—Tetsuya Kuroko. Kuroko's now a first-year high school student with zero presence who joins Seirin High's basketball club. Though his physical abilities and stats are well below average, Kuroko thrives on the court by making passes his opponents can't detect!

Seirin's aiming to qualify for Inter-High. So far, they've made their way through the qualifiers, taking down the North King, Seiho. Now, in the final qualifier game against the East King, Shutoku, Seirin is struggling against the Miracle Generation's number one shooter, Midorima, and his devastating three-pointers. Seirin pulls off a stunning comeback at the end, but Midorima might still be able to turn the tables on them in the final seconds!

STORY THUS FAR

Table of Contents

35TH QUARTER:
I Knew It 007

36TH QUARTER:
Let's...Play Again 027

37TH QUARTER:
Idiots Won't Win! 047

38TH QUARTER:
Couldn't Wait 067

39TH QUARTER:
Spitting Image 087

40TH QUARTER:
Don't Make Me Laugh 109

41ST QUARTER:
It's "Leg," Actually 129

42ND QUARTER:
Opening Act 149

43RD QUARTER:
I Got It 175

44TH QUARTER:
Not Her Style 197

45TH QUARTER:
Let's Do This! 217

46TH QUARTER:
Not Bad at All 239

47TH QUARTER:
Leave It to Us 259

48TH QUARTER:
Nothing but Lunatics 279

49TH QUARTER:
Let's End This 299

50TH QUARTER:
Your Basketball 319

51ST QUARTER:
One Thing I Won't Do!! 339

52ND QUARTER:
To a New Challenge 359

35TH QUARTER: I KNEW IT

NO WAY ...
TO COME THIS FAR ...
... ONLY TO LOSE ...?
SHUP
SHK...
SHUTOKU
6
10

NO STINKING WAY!
WE GOTTA WIN!!
YEAHHH
YOU'VE GOT ... TWO JUMPS LEFT.
MOVE, DAMN LEGS... I DON'T CARE IF YOU BREAK!!!
I WON'T LET IT END THIS WAY AFTER DRAGGING DOWN THE TEAM IN BOTH GAMES TODAY!!
WAIT, NO... HE'S REALLY GONNA JUMP!!
BUT HE'S GOTTA BE PAST HIS LIMIT!!!!
YEAHHH
AHHHHH!
TMP!

INDEED.
I THOUGHT AS MUCH.
I KNEW YOU'D PUSH PAST YOUR LIMIT AND JUMP ANYWAY.
...?!
SERIN
J-D
6
00:02
SHK

YEAHHH
KUROKO'S NOT THE ONLY SEASONED VETERAN HERE!
SHINTARO MIDORIMA ...
PUMP-FAKING IN THE FINAL SECONDS ?!
THIS IS THE MIRACLE GENERATION ...
HE'S SURE GOT GUTS.
HE GOT ME...
YEAHHH
END IT, MIDORIMA !!
YEAHHH
THE GAME'S OURS ...!!
NICE !!
I KNEW IT AS WELL...
KAGAMI-KUN WOULD JUMP...
...AND...
...KNOWING THAT, YOU WOULD LOWER THE BALL, MIDORIMA-KUN.

10
00:01

KU...
KURO-
KO
!!!

0:00

EIRI

HCH
THE GAME'S ...
HHH

VS
0:00
SEIRIN
SHUTOKU
1 2 3 4 TO OT
00:01
...OVER !!

YEAHHH
YEAHHH
YEAHHH
YEAHHH
YEAHHH
8

YEAHHH
YEAHHH
YEAHHH
YEAHHH
YEAHHH
GUESS THE HORO-SCOPE'S WRONG EVERY NOW AND THEN!
JUST SHUT UP.
C'MON... TIME TO LINE UP.

THANK YOU FOR THE GAME !!
WITH A SCORE OF 82 TO 81, SEIRIN HIGH SCHOOL WINS!!
SEIRIN
10
SHIRIN
4

I NEED TO GET SOME AIR.
HUH ?
DOESN'T HE FEEL ANYTHING AFTER A LOSS?
HM...
THERE'S NO TIME TO MOPE.
LET'S GROW STRONGER FROM TODAY'S LOSS.
IT'S PER-FECTLY NORMAL TO FEEL FRUSTRA-TION.
I BET HE'S NOT FEELING GOOD AT ALL.

FSSHHHH
NEXT UP IS THE FINALS LEAGUE.
IT WON'T BE LONG UNTIL WE PLAY AGAINST AOMINE-CHI.
RING RING

WELL, HOW'D IT GO?! THE GAME, I MEAN. YOU WIN?! LOSE?! AS FOR US, WE...
BEEP
AHH, MIDORIN, IT'S BEEN SOOO LONG!!
C'MON! ENOUGH ALREADY ...
BEEP
RING
RING
...THOSE TWO WERE DESTINED TO CLASH ON THE COURT.
I ALWAYS THOUGHT...
SIGH...
BEEP
NYAHH ?!
KLIK!!
YOU SHOULD BE CAREFUL IN THE FINALS LEAGUE.
YEAH...
OH YEAH?! YOU SERIOUS?! DON'T BE WEIRD.
SO GLOOMY, MAN. SO I'M GUESSING YOU, UH, LOST?!
AOMINE ?

THE ONLY GUY WHO CAN BEAT ME...
IF RIGHT NOW, KAGAMI IS THE LIGHT TO KUROKO-CHI'S SHADOW, THEN ...
YOU COULD SAY THAT AOMINE WAS THE LIGHT OF THE MIRACLE GENERATION.
FLASH
DAIKI AOMINE
Power Forward
6'4", 187 lbs

...IS ME.

KUROKO'S BASKETBALL BLOOPERS

TAKE 12

YOU HAVEN'T CHANGED, AOMINE.
HA...

YOU'RE MISUNDERSTANDING SOMETHING, MIDORIMA.
...
YOU'LL BE FACING KUROKO IN THE FINALS LEAGUE.
YOU UNDERSTAND WHAT I'M SAYING, RIGHT?

36TH QUARTER:
LET'S...PLAY AGAIN
THE PAST IS THE PAST.
NOW...
...HE'S A RIVAL.

AOMINE...

I'M HANGING UP.
SURE.
MIDORIN!! SORRY YOU'RE DOWN IN THE DUMPS!! CHEER UP.
SHAD-DUP!!
SIGH
KLIK
FSSHH

36TH QUARTER: LET'S...PLAY AGAIN

C'MON, KUROKO. JUST TRY A LITTLE HARD—
AHHHHHH!!!
NO. I'M AFRAID THIS IS TOO MUCH.
YOU SURE YOU CAN DO IT, KUROKO?
FSS
SHH...
LET'S DECIDE BY ROCK-PAPER-SCISSORS!
SOMEONE GIVE KAGAMI A PIGGYBACK RIDE!
FS SHH...
TEPPAN KITCHEN
OKONOM
SW
SORRY. YOU'RE TOO HEAVY.
I'LL REMEMBER THIS, KUROKO...
SOP...
PARDON US.
ELCOME
HM?

MM?
OH.
400円
SLZ
SLZ

TABLES FOR 15 OF US, PLEASE.
WE WERE WATCHING YOUR MATCH.
WHY'RE YOU TWO HERE ...?
CONGRATS ON MAKING IT!

WE'RE NOT THAT FAMIL-IAR!!
'SUP, MY MAN...?
KISE AND KASA-MATSU ?!

GAB
GAB
GAB
WE DON'T MIND SHARING A TABLE WITH OTHERS.
WAIT! DON'T JUST SEAT YOUR-SELVES ...
WE'LL JUST PACK OUR-SELVES IN.
I'M AFRAID WE DON'T HAVE ENOUGH SEATING.
WOW. THAT'S ONE LARGE PARTY.

...
SZZ....

PARDON US.
ALL RIGHT, EVERY-ONE ...
CHEERS!

WHY DO YOU ALL LOOK SO SAD?
AND WHY'RE YOU COVERED IN MUD, KAGAMI-CHI?
FORGET THE MUD. HOW'D WE END UP WITH YOU? AND DON'T USE "CHI" WITH ME.
IT'LL BURN IF YOU DON'T EAT IT.

COLA FOR ME!
ORANGE SODA!
LONG ISLAND ICED TEA HERE.
WHO'S THE MORON WHO ORDERED BOOZE? RETURN THAT!

SWF

TABLE...
...FOR TWO PLEASE ...
HM?
MENU

TEPPAN KITCHEN
OKONOM
FSSHHHHHHHHHH

LET'S FIND A DIFFERENT RESTAURANT, TAKAO.
HUH?

YOU TWO AS WELL?! WHERE'S THE REST OF YOUR TEAM?!
THEY LEFT US BEHIND WHEN SHIN-CHAN BROKE DOWN AND STARTED CRYING.
SO I THOUGHT WHY NOT GET SOME GRUB.
HEY

YOU'RE SHUTOKU'S...
AREN'T YOU KASAMATSU-SAN...FROM KAIJO?!
YOU KNOW ME?
I SAW YOU IN BASKETBALL MONTHLY. YOU'RE FAMOUS FOR BEING ONE OF THE BEST POINT GUARDS!

HM?

HOLD ON...! WE PLAY THE SAME POSITION. I'VE GOT A TON TO ASK YOU ABOUT !!
MIND IF WE JOIN YOU?!
UH...
WE'RE KIND OF CELEBRATING HERE...
IS YOU OKAY WITH THAT ?
OH, I DON'T MIND AT ALL!!
NOW THEN, KASAMATSU-SAN.
OVER HERE!!
OKAY... FEEL FREE.

RRMMBBB
SZZSZZ...
THIS IS BEYOND EXCITING, ISN'T IT?!
YOU WANTED THIS, DIDN'T YOU?
WHO? LITTLE OLD ME? ♡
SPARKLE
BADUM BADUM
HEH-HEH
LOOKIT THAT LINEUP !!
BA M

I'M QUITE HUNGRY.
ANYHOW, WHAT SHOULD WE ORDER?
MENU
SZZ...
SZZ...
YOU DON'T GOTTA PUT IT LIKE THAT!!
ONLY YOU WOULD INSIST ON EATING SOMETHING SO GROSS.
BLRF
SIGH...
I'M ALREADY PRETTY FULL.
WHAT I'VE GOT HERE NOW IS ENOUGH FOR ME.
SQUID, PORK, MIXED PLATE, OCTOPUS, PORK KIMCHEE...
YOU CHANTING A CURSE OVER THERE ?!
THAT'S TOO MUCH !!
DON'T WORRY. KAGAMI-KUN WILL EAT IT ALL BY HIMSELF.
IS HE HUMAN ?!

SIZZL...

I GET IT. YOU'RE SAD YOU LOST, BUT...
C'MON! YESTERDAY'S ENEMY IS TODAY'S... SOMETHING OR OTHER.
A LOSS IS A LOSS. I'M ALREADY PAST THAT!

MIDORIMACHI. YOUR FOOD'S BURNING.
I DON'T FEEL VERY MUCH LIKE EATING RIGHT NOW.

OH, THAT ...

WHAT I FAIL TO UNDERSTAND IS WHY YOU'RE SITTING SO CAREFREE AT THE SAME TABLE...
...WITH THE VERY SAME RIVALS WHO BEAT YOU!

THAT'S BECAUSE I'LL STILL GET MY REVENGE...
...ON THE INTER-HIGH STAGE!

YEAH.
THAT'S WHAT I WANNA HEAR.

GULP

I WON'T LOSE AGAIN.

KISE...
YOU'VE CHANGED A BIT.
THAT SO?
YOUR EYES... ARE STRANGE.
STRANGE ?!

WELL... EVER SINCE LOSING TO KUROKO-CHI'S TEAM...
...I'VE ACTUALLY BEEN PRACTICING. UNLIKE BEFORE...
BEYOND THAT...
I'M FINALLY HAVING FUN PLAYING BASKETBALL WITH MY BUDDIES AT KAIJO.

YOU'VE ONLY RE-GRESSED ...
...TO A TIME BEFORE WE WERE THREE-TIME CHAMPS.
THEN I WAS UTTERLY MISTAKEN.
YOU HAVEN'T CHANGED AT ALL.

YOU ALL CAN CHANGE HOWEVER YOU WANT.
BUT WHEN I PLAY BASKETBALL, FUN IS NOT A FACTOR.

NOM...
...

BUT...
IT'S NOT LIKE WE WERE ALL LIKE THAT, BACK THEN.

WHAT'D YOU SAY ...?
OF COURSE YOU'RE SUPPOSED TO PLAY BASKETBALL CUZ IT'S FUN.
YOU GUYS THINK WAY TOO HARD ABOUT THIS JUNK.

I'LL ASK YOU NOT TO SPEAK ON MATTERS YOU'RE COMPLETELY IGNORANT ABOUT.

WE'LL HAVE THAT TALK LATER.
SHAH

...
TWINGE

SPLAT!
AH!

I THOUGHT THAT DURING THE GAME TODAY.
IT'S JUST AS YOU SAID, KAGAMI-KUN.

GET OVER HERE, TAKAO.
SORRY, SORRY... SERIOUSLY, DUDE, SORRY... WHAT'RE YOU DOING WITH THAT *OKONO-MIYAKI*...?
EEK!!
KRASH!!

IF WE HADN'T BEEN ENJOYING IT, WE NEVER WOULD HAVE PLAYED SO HARD.

OH.
LOOKS LIKE THE RAIN LET UP.
YOU'RE RIGHT.
WELL, THIS WAS FUN. ABOUT TIME TO HEAD HOME, THOUGH.

THERE ARE TWO MEMBERS OF THE MIRACLE GENERATION IN TOKYO.
MYSELF AND ONE OTHER...
DAIKI AOMINE.
I EXPECT YOU'LL FACE HIM IN THE FINALS LEAGUE.
KAGAMI. LET ME GIVE YOU ONE WARNING.
SHAH

YOU SHOULD KNOW ...
...THAT HE'S THE SAME TYPE OF PLAYER AS YOU.

YOU'RE BASICALLY JUST SAYING HE'S GOOD?
HUH?
THE HELL'S THAT S'POSED TO MEAN ...?

YES. HE'S GOOD.
BUT THE WAY HE PLAYS BASKET-BALL...
I DON'T LIKE IT.
...

ANYHOW, DO YOUR BEST AGAINST HIM.
MIDORIMA-KUN...!
HMPH...

SURE, BUT NEXT TIME...
I'LL WIN!
LET'S...
...PLAY EACH OTHER AGAIN SOMEDAY.

OKONON
NO NEED TO PLAY ROCK-PAPER-SCISSORS TO SEE WHO PEDALS THIS TIME.

CLATTER...

WHAT'D YOU SAY ?!
EITHER WAY, IT'S ALWAYS YOU WHO LOSES, TAKAO.

HMPH ...

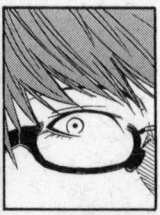

NEXT TIME, I'LL JUST HAVE TO PURCHASE A LARGER PIECE OF POTTERY.
NO MORE MISTAKES FROM HERE ON OUT.
WHAT ABOUT THAT WHOLE LUCKY-ITEM THING ...?
NO NEED TO STATE THE OBVIOUS.
ANYWAY, WE'LL BEAT 'EM NEXT TIME.
IT'S NOT ABOUT THE SIZE !!
DING DING...
CLATTER
CLATTER
CLATTER

LET'S HEAD OUT!
SEIRIN
NEXT UP... THE FINALS LEAGUE !!
YEAHHH !!
SEIRIN HIGH SCHOOL IS THE WINNER OF A-BLOCK IN INTER-HIGH'S TOKYO QUALIFIER TOURNAMENT.
THEY MOVE ON TO THE FINALS LEAGUE!!
SO MUCH !!
50,000 YEN...?!
HOW MUCH DID THAT BONE-HEAD KAGAMI EAT?
FOOTING THE BILL

KUROKO'S BASKETBALL TAKE 3 BLOOPERS

37TH QUARTER: IDIOTS WON'T WIN!

ON THE FINAL DAY OF THE INTER-HIGH QUALIFIERS TOURNAMENT, A-BLOCK ...

SEIRIN'S SEMI-FINAL MATCH WAS AGAINST SEIHO HIGH, THE NORTH KING.

SEIRIN STRUGGLED AGAINST SEIHO'S DEFENSE, WHICH INCORPORATED ANCIENT MARTIAL ARTS TECHNIQUES, BUT THE SECOND-YEARS TAPPED INTO THEIR HIDDEN POTENTIAL AND PULLED OFF A WIN.

THE FINAL MATCH WAS AGAINST SHUTOKU HIGH, THE EAST KING.

MIDORIMA OF THE MIRACLE GENERATION AND HIS DEVASTATING THREE-POINTERS OVERWHELMED THE TEAM AT FIRST, BUT KUROKO AND A RE-ENERGIZED KAGAMI MANAGED TO PULL OFF AN IMPRESSIVE COMEBACK VICTORY.

TOKYO INTER-HIGH QUALIFIERS FINALS LEAGUE

	SEIRIN	B-BLOCK WINNER	C-BLOCK WINNER	D-BLOCK WINNER
A-BLOCK WINNER: SEIRIN				
B-BLOCK WINNER: ?				
C-BLOCK WINNER: ?				
D-BLOCK WINNER: ?				

SEIRIN FACED AN UPHILL BATTLE BY PLAYING TWO OF THE THREE KINGS, TOKYO'S ELITE SCHOOLS, IN ONE DAY. HOWEVER, THEY EMERGED AS THE WINNERS OF THE TOURNAMENT'S A-BLOCK.

SEIRIN HAS REACHED THE FINALS LEAGUE, THE LAST BATTLE STANDING BETWEEN THEM AND INTER-HIGH.

*THE TOP THREE OF FOUR MOVE ON TO INTER-HIGH.

HOW-EVER ...

数学

OH! AS I'M SURE YOU ALL KNOW...
THAT'S ALL FOR TODAY.
DING DONG
DING DONG

TWITCH...
ONE OTHER OBSTACLE LAY AHEAD.
MAKE SURE YOU STUDY HARD IN ALL YOUR SUBJECTS.
TWO DAYS FROM NOW, YOU'LL HAVE YOUR PROFICIENCY TESTS.

37TH QUARTER:

IDIOTS WON'T WIN!

SHEESH...
COACH IS ALWAYS ON OUR BUTTS ABOUT SOMETHING.

THIS TIME IT'S "BRING ME ALL YOUR MID-TERMS"...
I BET SHE'S COMING UP WITH SOME WEIRD SCHEME AGAIN.
OR MAYBE IT'S JUST EXACTLY WHAT IT SEEMS LIKE.

FURI-HATA...
KAWA-HARA...
...AND... FUKUDA !!
HEY, YOU FINALLY REMEM-BERED OUR NAMES!
YEAH.

HEY, KAGAMI!

HUH? REALLY ?
BUT THESE UPCOMING PROFICIENCY TESTS DON'T AFFECT OUR GRADES, RIGHT?
I'VE HEARD THAT KIDS WHO FAIL CAN'T COMPETE IN INTER-HIGH. MAYBE IT'S THAT...
STILL, A LITTLE EARLY, NO?
WHADDYA THINK THIS IS ALL ABOUT?
YEAH.
YOU GUYS BROUGHT YOUR OLD TESTS TOO?

SHOULDN'T WE BE PRACTICING BASKETBALL INSTEAD?
MY MUSCLES ARE STILL SORE AS HECK, THOUGH...
THEN THERE'S REALLY NO PROBLEM!

THERE DEFINITELY IS...
...A PROBLEM!

THE BOTTOM HUNDRED HAVE TO ATTEND EXTRA LESSONS STARTING NEXT SATURDAY.
THAT'S WHERE THE PROBLEM COMES IN.
HM...
OH!

SURE, THESE TESTS DON'T AFFECT YOUR GRADES...
BUT...
THERE'RE 300 KIDS IN EACH GRADE AT OUR SCHOOL...
...AND THESE TESTS DETERMINE OUR RANKINGS.

SATURDAY... THE FINALS LEAGUE!!
YEP.
SO IF YOU BOMB THESE TESTS, YOU'RE OUT OF THE GAME.
HUHHHH...

SO THEN, IF WE DECIDE YOU'RE ON THIN ICE BASED ON YOUR MIDTERM SCORES...
...THEN YOU'LL BE ATTENDING CRAM SESSIONS STARTING TONIGHT AT COACH'S HOUSE.
SHE'S GOT THE BIGGEST PLACE.
AT COACH'S HOUSE ...?
TWITCH
JUST FOR STUDYING. NOTHING ELSE...

EEEP!!
DON'T GO THINKING WITH YOUR MINDS IN THE GUTTER, ESPECIALLY YOU IDIOTS DUMB ENOUGH TO POTENTIALLY MISS A GAME...
WHRR

JUST BE SURE TO STUDY LIKE NORMAL.
LOOKS LIKE YOU'LL BE FINE.
HM...

THE FUTURE OF SEIRIN'S BASKETBALL PROGRAM IS RIDING ON THIS!!
THE TWO WE ABSOLUTELY CAN'T DO WITHOUT IN THE FINALS LEAGUE...!
BADUM
BADUM
BADUM
OKAY. FIRST, KUROKO-KUN.

OF COURSE!!
THE ONLY TWO LEFT ARE...
YO.
HELLO.

Math I
Tetsuya Kuroko
59
Chemistry
1 Class B # 6
Tetsuya Kuroko
49
55
Japanese History
Class
1 8 6
Tetsuya Kuroko
63
81
JAPANESE ANSWER SHEET

HE'S SO AVERAGE.
WAHHHH...

OH NO
DON'T TELL ME ...?!

HUNH ?!
KUROKO, YOU... WHO KNEW YOU WERE SUCH A BRAINIAC ...?
GULP!

N-NOT BAD, I GUESS.
BUT NOT REALLY GOOD, EITHER!!
AH, BUT... HE'S OKAY IN JAPANESE!
GREAT!
BUT STILL, REALLY AVERAGE!
...

RRMBBB

Biology

Class B # 7 Taiga Kagami

41

0

3

14

JAPANESE ANSWER SHEET

一年

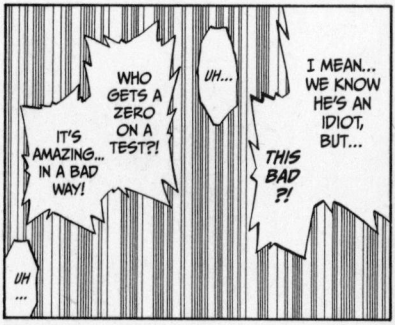

ARGH! LOOKS LIKE WE'LL ALL HAVE TO PITCH IN AND TUTOR THIS GUY.
DON'T TALK BACK TO YOUR ELDERS.
FWIP
THE ENGLISH WE LEARN HERE'S WAY TOO TEXT-BOOK!!
IT'S DIFFERENT THAN HAVING A NORMAL CONVER-SATION!!
DIDN'T YOU LIVE ABROAD UNTIL RECENTLY ?!
HOW'D YOU EVEN FLUNK ENGLISH ?!
OF COURSE.
NERDIER THAN YOU, AT LEAST.
WHAM
DON'T LOOK DOWN ON US.
YOU MEAN YOU'RE ALL NERDY ENOUGH TO ACTUALLY TEACH THIS STUFF?
HUH ...?
B AM
Previous Proficiency Test Rankings (305 Total Students)
2nd Place
52nd Place
71st Place
74th Place
81st Place
112th Place

...
SHOCK

SLAP!!
IF I'M GOOD AT BASKET-BALL, WHO CARES ABOUT ACADEM-ICS...
OW!

NOT EVERYONE WITH GLASSES IS SMART!! BETTER THAN AVERAGE IS GOOD ENOUGH!!
BUT THE CAPTAIN... I THOUGHT HE'D BE HIGHER SINCE HE WEARS GLASSES AND ALL...
UH... WHOA... COACH... YOU WERE SECOND?! YOU'RE THAT SMART?!

BAM
BUT IDIOTS WON'T WIN!
ANY IDIOT CAN PLAY BASKET-BALL!
ZING

...
SHOCK

THE PROFICIENCY TESTS CONSIST OF FIVE SUBJECTS!!
SINCE EACH OF US HERE EXCELS IN AT LEAST ONE SUBJECT...
...WE'VE ASSEMBLED A SPECIAL TUTORING TEAM FOR YOU!
English (Reading Passages, Grammar)
Social Studies (Japanese History, World History, Geography)
Math (Math I, Math A)
Japanese (Modern, Classical, Kanji)
Science (Physics, Chemistry, Biology)
Supreme Commander
Kadummy's Academic Improvement Special Tutoring Team
BA
WHIP...
M.

KOGANEI'S NOT GREAT OR TERRIBLE AT ANY SUBJECT!
AN ACADEMIC JACK-OF-ALL-TRADES!
I GET TO WHACK YOU IF YOU FALL ASLEEP!
BAM!
SHP
WHAT ABOUT YOU, KOGANEI?

NOT MUCH TIME?! HOW 'BOUT NONE AT ALL?!
KADUMMY'S ACADEMIC IMPROVEMENT STRATEGY
(16th, 6 A.M.)
STUDY
9 A.M.
SCHOOL (STUDYING)
12
(15th, 6 P.M.)
(16th, 6 P.M.)
3 P.M.
STUDY!!
SCHOOL
TEST
STUDY!!!
9 A.M.
(17th, 6 A.M.)
(17th)
THERE WON'T BE MUCH TIME FOR SLEEP GOING FORWARD !!
BAM!!
SHOCK

I WANNA GO HOME !!
WE'LL START WITH MATH !!
AND NO ONE EVER DIED FROM TWO DAYS WITH NO SLEEP!
GROW UP! ADULTS DON'T COMPLAIN ABOUT EFFICIENCY !!
HOLD ON... DOESN'T PULLING ALL-NIGHTERS AFFECT EFFICIENCY ...?

MURMUR
MURMUR
MURMUR-MURMUR
GLOOM

KAGAMI, WE'LL BE STUDYING IN THE LIBRARY AT LUNCH.
RIGHT...

ARE YOU OKAY?
GONNA DIE...

OH.
I GAVE IT TO HIM.
YOUR NUMBER...
YOU DID?!
DON'T GO AROUND DOING THAT!!

HOW'RE KISE AND MIDORIMA WHEN IT COMES TO SCHOOL?
MIDORIMA-KUN IS SMART.
KISE-KUN, LESS SO.
...

SHAH...
I'M SERIOUSLY GONNA DIE.
OH. AND KISE TEXTED ME YESTERDAY.

From: Ryota Kise
Subject: Earlier
Forgot to mention, but I'm heading to Inter-High too. Can't wait to get revenge!!
ANYWAY, HERE'S HIS TEXT...

IF WE DON'T WIN AT THE FINALS LEAGUE, NO INTER-HIGH FOR US. EVEN IF WE DO WIN THERE, INTER-HIGH'LL BE A BUST IF I'M TOO DUMB FOR THESE TESTS.
SO IF I WANNA BEAT THE MIRACLE GENERATION AND BE THE BEST IN JAPAN...
...I CAN'T AFFORD TO SCREW UP HERE!
SWAY

MIDORIMA-KUN GAVE IT TO ME LONG AGO. IT'LL BE YOUR LAST RESORT.
IT'S A MAGICAL DICE-ROLL PENCIL FROM YUSHIMA TENJIN SHRINE.
DON'T NEED IT!!
TOSS

HOWEVER THINGS TURN OUT, I WANT YOU TO HAVE THIS...
WUZ-ZAT?
ROLL

KAGAMI-KUN...

JUST ONE LAST SUBJECT... YOU CAN'T SEEM TO IMPROVE AT JAPANESE...
WHAT A DRAG...
SIGHooo
TICK
TICK...
YOU'RE TERRIBLE AT KANJI.
AND YOU CAN'T DEAL WITH READING PASSAGES.
CLASSICAL LIT IS A LOST CAUSE...
?
?
I KNOW!
LET'S TRY THIS...
CHIRP CHIRP
THESE TESTS ARE ALL MULTIPLE-CHOICE WITH FOUR OPTIONS.
JUST GUESS, AND YOU'RE BOUND TO GET AROUND 25 PERCENT!
YOU'LL MAKE UP FOR IT WITH THE OTHER FOUR SUBJECTS !!
SERIOUSLY ...?
TWEET TWEET
JUST WING IT, FOR JAPANESE!
WHA-?!
GLOOM

JUST LIKE I THOUGHT ...

SKRITCH
SKRITCH
SKRITCH
SKRITCH

SKRITCH
SKRITCH
SKRITCH
SKRITCH
SKRITCH

I'M NOT GONNA PASS IN ANY OF THESE SUBJECTS!
FORGET SACRI-FICING ONE SUBJECT
GLOOM

I CAN DO IT!
BAM
NO! AFTER ALL THAT STUDYING, I CAN'T GIVE UP!
SKRITCH
SKRITCH

...
JAPANESE— MY WORST SUBJECT
...
NOT TO MENTION THE FINAL ONE
...
SECOND PERIOD: SCIENCE 9:00 ~ 9:50
THIRD PERIOD: MATH 10:00 ~ 10:50
(LUNCH) 11:00 ~ 11:50
FOURTH PERIOD: SOCIAL STUDIES 13:00 ~ 13:50
FIFTH PERIOD: JAPANESE 14:00 ~ 14:50

...

KAGAMI-KUN... DON'T TELL ME...
CRAM IT.
I'VE BEEN ROLLING A PENCIL TO RANDOMLY PICK ANSWERS FOR FIFTY MINUTES STRAIGHT.
I'M DEAD.
WORMP...

WELL...

THE NEXT DAY...
KAGAMI! HOW'D THE TESTS GO?

WHA
HUHA ?!
HOW ?!
WAIT, WHAT?! A 98 PERCENT ON JAPANESE ?!
WHAT ?!
?!
FWIP
FIRST SEMESTER PROFICIENCY TEST RESULTS
Taiga Kagami
90th
308 students

IT'S MIDORIMA-KUN'S MAGICAL DICE-ROLL PENCIL.

I... UH... JUST ROLLED THAT PENCIL TO GET THE ANSWERS ...
HOW'D YOU PULL IT OFF ...?!
FOR REAL ?!

KAGAMI ALSO WEPT...
...FOR HE FELT HE HAD LOST TO MIDO-RIMA.
I ENDED UP NEEDING HELP FROM THAT GUY...
HYUGA WEPT THAT DAY...
...FOR HE HAD SOME-HOW LOST TO KAGAMI.
AT LEAST I'M NOT STUPID...
EVERYONE MANAGED TO GET OUT OF THE SUPPLE-MENTARY LESSONS.
HOW-EVER ...
WHAT THE HECK?! MIDORIMA'S WEIRD!!

KUROKO'S BASKETBALL BLOOPERS

TAKE 1

38TH QUARTER: COULDN'T WAIT

GOOO ...
SEIRIN !!
YEAHHH !!

38TH QUARTER: COULDN'T WAIT

SHK
SHK
SHK
SHK
SEIRIN'S PRACTICES ALWAYS EMPHASIZE THE FUNDAMENTALS.
LAST TEN!!
YEAH !!
FOOT-WORK. SHOOTING. PASSING.
THEY DRILL ON ALL THE BASIC MOVES.
SHK
ACTUALLY KINDA GLAD I GET TO SIT THIS ONE OUT...
FWIP
FWIP
SIDE-LINED DUE TO LEG INJURIES FROM THE SHUTOKU GAME
NO SLEEPING, KUROKO !!
HAHH
HAHH
HAHH
THEIR PRACTICES ARE JUST AS LONG AND INTENSE AS ANY ELITE CHAMPIONSHIP SCHOOL.
IT'S VERY HARSH.
HAHH
HAHH

BAP
SHK
THROW IT INTO THE POST!!
LOOK AROUND YOU.
THOUGH THEY DON'T FOCUS AS MUCH ON PRACTICING SET PLAYS AND SCRIMMAGES...
...THE PRACTICES ARE ALWAYS INTENSE WITH A HEAVY FOCUS ON FUNDAMENTALS.
KEEP YOUR HANDS UP.
SHK
BAP
SHK

THE TEAM USES DIFFERENT TYPES OF BALLS.
THIS IS MEANT TO LIMIT MOVEMENT AND IMPROVE THEIR ABILITY TO ADAPT.
THESE OTHER BALLS CAN BE LARGER OR SMALLER THAN A REGULATION BASKET-BALL.
IN THE MOST EXTREME CASE, THEY EVEN USE A TENNIS BALL.
LARGE

THE TEAM ENDS PRACTICE WITH A SCRIMMAGE AND A TEAM MEETING.
AND THEN ...

SWISH
SHK
EACH PLAYER WORKS OUT ON HIS OWN.
FWIP
SHK
THIS PART ISN'T MANDATORY.
HOWEVER, THE BETTER THE PLAYER, THE MORE TIME THEY SPEND ON THIS.
SHP
BAP
SHK
SHK
BA

CLANG...

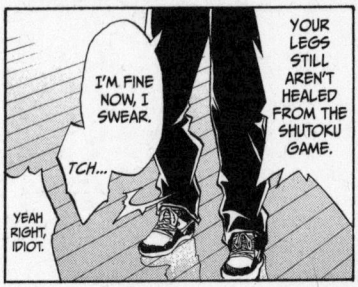
YOUR LEGS STILL AREN'T HEALED FROM THE SHUTOKU GAME.
I'M FINE NOW, I SWEAR.
TCH...
YEAH RIGHT, IDIOT.

WATCHING EVERYONE, I COULDN'T RESIST.
AH!
NO PRACTICE FOR YOU, KAGAMI! NOT YET!!

HM?

WHACK
KEEP THIS UP, AND IT'LL BECOME A BAD HABIT. SO KNOCK IT OFF!
OUCH!!
PRACTICING WHEN YOU'RE TOLD TO SIT OUT DOESN'T MEAN YOU'RE SERIOUS.

OH, HYUGA-KUN! I'LL TEXT EVERYONE LATER.
YOU-KNOW-WHERE IS CLOSED TO THE PUBLIC TOMORROW, SO WE'LL BE DOING YOU-KNOW-WHAT.
OKAY!

LUCKILY, THE TOURNAMENT ORGANIZERS HAVE SET THE FINALS LEAGUE FOR TWO WEEKS FROM NOW...
...SO YOU GET A WHOLE WEEK TO REST THOSE LEGS!
DON'T BOTHER COMING IN TOMORROW, EITHER. IT'S SATURDAY.

SPORTS GYM
BE SURE TO STRETCH EVEN MORE THAN NORMAL.
THIS IS SEIRIN'S BASKETBALL CLUB'S INFAMOUS POOL TRAINING.
WE'LL START WITH SQUATS!
RUNA
FWEE
SPLASH
SPLASH
SPLASH
THE GYM THAT RIKA AIDA'S FATHER MANAGES...
...IS JUST A TEN-MINUTE WALK FROM SEIRIN HIGH.

THREE EARLY MORNINGS A WEEK, BEFORE THE GYM EVEN OPENS...
...THE TEAM GOES THROUGH FOOTWORK DRILLS AND MUSCLE TRAINING INSTEAD OF THE USUAL MORNING PRACTICE.
BLUB—
NO SLEEPING, KUROKO !!
I MEAN, NO FLOATING!!
...A LIVING HELL.
AT THE SAME TIME, THOUGH, THE WATER RESISTANCE MAKES THIS TRAINING...
WHEEZE
WHEEZE
WHEEZE
WHEEZE
THERE ARE WEIGHT MACHINES, OF COURSE...
...BUT THE HIGH SCHOOLERS, WITH THEIR STILL-GROWING BODIES, DON'T USE THEM FOR FEAR OF INJURY.
CONVERSELY, THE BUOYANCY PROVIDED BY THE WATER LESSENS THE CHANCE OF INJURY.
WHAT AN INTEREST-ING TRAINING METHOD.
Training Chart Pool Training
GIGGLE
GIGGLE
GREAT. REST FOR ONE MINUTE.
40!
50!!
GAH! THIS IS SERIOUS-LY HARSH !!
SPLA SH
SPLA SH

?!

BUH?!

UM... WHO ARE YOU?
THE GYM'S CLOSED TODAY...
WELL...
HOW DO I PUT THIS?

MOMOI-SAN...
FRIEND OF YOURS ?!

TETSU-KUN?
TETSUYA KUROKO-KUN. ♡

I'M TETSU-KUN'S GIRL-FRIEND. ♡
I COULDN'T WAIT UNTIL THE FINALS LEAGUE TO SEE HIM.

HUHHHHHHH...

AT TEIKO ...?!
...IS SHE WITH OUR NEXT OPPONENT ?!
WAIT. SHE SAID THE FINALS LEAGUE, SO...
YOU'VE GOT A GIRL-FRIEND, KUROKO ?!
NO, I DON'T.
SHE WAS JUST THE TEAM MANAGER DURING MIDDLE SCHOOL.
SPLASH
GLOM~P
IT'S BEEN SO LONG. I'VE MISSED YOU!!
THAT HURTS, MOMOI-SAN.
SHAH
!
TETSU-KUN?!
SH~UP
WHA~?!
GOOD GOING, KUROKO! BUT I HOPE YOU DIE!!
WE'RE JEALOUS, KUROKO!!
NO CLUE WHAT'S GOING ON HERE, BUT ...

THAT'S FINE.
BESIDES, HE'S A TOTALLY DIFFERENT MAN ON THE COURT. BRAVE AND DASHING, DON'TCHA THINK?
HUH?
HE'S SO DULL AND SMALL AND WIMPY.
HOLD ON... W-W-WHY KUROKO ?!
...
HRMMM

GAB
GAB
GAB
ALSO... HE GAVE ME A POPSICLE.
HUH ?!

TAKE WHAT...? YOUR GARBAGE? YUCK.
WHAT A JERK.
WHAT'S UP WITH HIM...?
HUH?
HERE, TAKE THIS.
I DON'T NEED IT.
MAYBE A POPSICLE LIKE EVERYONE ELSE...?
WHAT SHOULD I GET...?

WINNER

HUH?! YOU GAVE IT TO HER? WHAT A WASTE!!
I'M ALREADY FULL.

CHAK

WHAT A WEIRD DEVELOPMENT...
MOMOI-SAN...
NOT SO LOUD IN THE POOL AREA, PLEASE. IT ECHOES IN HERE.
BUT... BUT...
I REALLY WANTED TO GO TO THE SAME SCHOOL AS YOU, TETSU-KUN, BUT...!!
WAHHHH!

?

YOU'RE ALL JUST GETTING WORKED UP CUZ SHE'S *KINDA* CUTE WITH KINDA BIG BOOBS!
HEH...
RIGHT, HYUGA-KUN?

W...
W-W-W...
WHAT'S UP WITH THIS CHICK ?!
CHATTER
CHATTER
CHATTER

RIGHT...
GLANCE
SURE...

YOU'VE GONE AND KILLED HYUGA-SAN.
STOP PEEKING AT THOSE MELONS!!
ALL YOU MEN ARE THE SAME— ROTTEN!!
P
OW
UH...
HOW DO YOU KNOW MY NAME ...?

YOU'RE SEIRIN'S CLUTCH-SHOOTING BASKETBALL CAPTAIN...
HYUGA-SAN.
WHY WOULDN'T I?

KOGANEI-SAN...
...AND TSUCHIDA-SAN.
HUH?! THAT'S ALL WE GET?!
SHOCK!!

THE SILENT PRO-FESSIONAL WITH A MEAN HOOK SHOT...
MITOBE-SAN.

THEN THERE'S YOUR POINT GUARD WITH THE EAGLE EYE...
IZUKI-SAN.

MOMOI-SAN...
AREN'T YOU AT THE SAME SCHOOL AS AOMINE-KUN?

WHO IS THIS CHICK?!
IRK

WHAT THE HELL?!
HOW DO YOU KNOW SO MUCH?!
RIKO-SAN.
AND THE JUST-BARELY-B-CUP COACH...
GACK!

MM-HMM...

BAP...
BAP

SWISH!

I KNOW COACH SAID TO REST...
EXCITED
...BUT I JUST CAN'T SIT STILL.
BAP

I REALLY WANTED TO GO TO THE SAME SCHOOL AS YOU, TETSU-KUN...
...BUT...

OOH, YOU'RE REALLY HERE.
SATSUKI'S INTEL GATHERING IS SOME-THING ELSE.
...?!
ROLL

YEAH, MOST OF THE PAIN IS GONE ...
OUCH ?!

...IF I LEFT *HIM* ON HIS OWN...
TAIGA KAGAMI... RIGHT?
...THERE'D BE NO TELLING WHAT TROUBLE HE MIGHT CAUSE...

SHAK
PLAY ME.
I WANNA TEST YOUR SKILLS.
HUH ?
WHO THE HELL'RE YOU?

KUROKO'S BASKETBALL BLOOPERS

TAKE 2

39TH QUARTER: SPITTING IMAGE

WHO THE HELL'RE YOU?
DON'T TELL ME TO PLAY YOU WITHOUT INTRODUCING YOURSELF FIRST.
SCREW THAT!
I DIDN'T ASK HOW YOU FELT ABOUT IT.
I SAID "PLAY ME," SO LET'S DO IT.
BUT...I GUESS I'LL TELL YOU MY NAME.
IT'S DAIKI AOMINE.
OKAY?
AOMINE...?!
HE'S ONE OF THE MIRACLE GENERATION GUYS WE'RE FACING IN THE FINALS LEAGUE...!

HA HA.
HEY!
HEY!
BUT IT'S NOT LIKE I'D AGREE TO PLAY SOMEONE ACTING ALL HIGH AND MIGHTY...
GOOD TO KNOW.

LIKE I SAID, I WANNA TEST YOU.
DON'T THINK I ASK JUST ANYONE TO PLAY ME.
THE LESS POINTLESS CHITCHAT, THE BETTER.
THAT'S WHY I DIDN'T BOTHER TELLING YOU.

I JUST WANNA SEE HOW MUCH YOU CAN EASE MY BOREDOM.
I'M NOT GOING AROUND LOOKING FOR MY EQUAL.
THERE'S NO ONE STRONGER THAN ME.

FIRST KISE, THEN MIDORIMA...
ALL YOU MIRACLE GENERATION JERKS KNOW HOW TO GET ON MY NERVES.

HMPH ...

BUT YOU'VE EVEN GOT THEM BEAT IN THAT DEPARTMENT.
I'LL CRUSH YOU.
SNAP...

WHAT'S WITH KUROKO'S MANAGER FROM MIDDLE SCHOOL?
I WONDER ...

FS SS
GAH! MY WHOLE BODY'S WORN OUT.
HOW'RE WE SUPPOSED TO DO AFTERNOON PRACTICE AT THIS RATE?
HHHH...

GYM

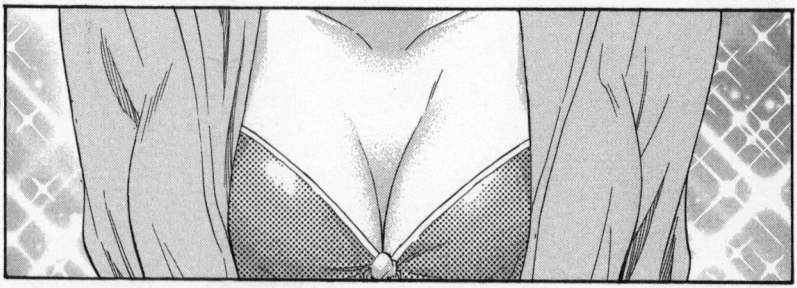

AFTERNOON PRACTICE WILL BE THREE TIMES AS HARSH TODAY.
RRMBBB...
WAIT, WHAT?! ARE YOU TRYING TO KILL US?
YES. INDEED I AM.
WHA-?!

NICE...
BADUM
BADUM
BADUM

YOUR TEAM TOO, MOMOI-SAN.
SO YOU'RE IN THE FINALS LEAGUE? CONGRATS!
...

YES.
HA HA HA. I DID? REALLY?
AH.
YES, YOU DID.
OH? DID I MENTION THAT?

YES.
...WE'LL BE ON OPPOSITE BENCHES.
SO THE NEXT TIME WE MEET...

THAT... KAGAMI, WAS IT ?
IT WAS REALLY AMAZING.
I SAW THE REPLAY OF YOUR GAME AGAINST MIDORIN.

HE'S...
...THE SPITTING IMAGE OF *HIM*, FROM WAY BACK.

...
YES...

SITTING POOLSIDE WITH YOU LIKE THIS...
IT BRINGS BACK MEMORIES.
YOU TWO WERE ALWAYS THE MOST IN SYNC WITHIN THE MIRACLE GENERATION GUYS...
YEAHH!!
SWISH
©Senoh

YEAHHH
NICE!!
AWESOME PASS, TETSU!
YEAHHH
YEAHHH

SHK
ASK THE CAP-TAIN, THEN.
PFFT!
C'MON, KUROKO-CHI. PASS TO ME ONCE IN A WHILE!
SHK
AS ALWAYS, PRECISE ENOUGH TO MAKE ME DESPISE YOU.
HA HA.

IT MUST BE BECAUSE KUROKO IS A SHADOW.
I WONDER...
HUH ?

IT'S REALLY TRUE, ISN'T IT?
NOTHING REALLY SUITS YOU, TETSU, BUT...
...THE ONE THING YOU SINK YOUR TEETH INTO IS BASKET-BALL.

THE STRONGER THE LIGHT, THE DARKER THE SHADOW.
KUROKO'S TRUE STRENGTH EMERGES WHEN HE'S TEAMED UP WITH STRONG PLAYERS.
IT'S NOT AS IF KUROKO DOESN'T MESH WITH ANY OF US IN PARTICULAR.

HOW-EVER...
HE'S STRONGEST WITH *HIM*.
KUROKO'S TALENTS ARE ABLE TO EMERGE...
...BECAUSE *HIS* LIGHT SHINES SO VERY BRIGHT.
15
6
BUMP
...
BAP
ONE!
BAP...
SHK
SHK
SHK

To-oh Academy
Basketball Club
Point Guard, 5'11"
SHOICHI IMAYOSHI

SHK
WHAT TO DO ABOUT HIM...
OH BOY.
SIGH...
HE RAN OFF SOME-WHERE EARLIER.
HUH? WHERE'S AOMINE?
SKIPPING PRACTICE. AGAIN.
SHK
SHK
HUH?
UH? AH! YES?
SORRY.
HEY!
SAKU-RA!
HE'S IN MY CLASS, SO I SHOULD'VE STOPPED HIM...
...BUT I FAILED...
I'M SO SORRY... FOR LIVING.
NAH, THAT'S OKAY. NO BIG...
YOU'RE SORRY FOR LIVING ?!
PAUL
Shooting Guard
5'9"
RYO SAKURAI

SORRY, SORRY.
I'M SUCH A LOWLY WORM!
WORM ?!
YOU'RE TOO HARD ON YOUR-SELF.
NO, SERIOUSLY, IT'S FINE.
ACK! SORRY!
SORRY FOR BEING TOO HARD ON MY-SELF!
YOU'RE ANNOY-ING!!
SHK
MOMOI'S NOT HERE EITHER.
YEAH. THAT'S OKAY, THOUGH.
SHK
I BET SHE'S JUST HARD AT WORK.
SHK
AOMINE-KUN...
THE PLAYS HE MADE WITH YOU BACK THEN...
THOSE WERE SOME-THING ELSE.

...BUT HE NEVER LOSES.
EVEN BY HIMSELF... NOBODY CAN STOP HIM...

BUT NOW IT'S LIKE HE'S PLAYING ALL ALONE...
...ISOLATED FROM THE REST OF THE TEAM.
I'M SURE THINGS WOULD CHANGE IF HE LOST A GAME...

AH, SORRY.
TALKING ABOUT THE PAST, THINGS ALWAYS GET KINDA DARK...
WOULD AOMINE-KUN CHANGE ...
HUH ?

HUH ...?!
BUT...
I KNOW HOW GOOD AOMINE-KUN IS.
BUT...

...IF I WERE TO STOP HIM?

IT'S NOT AS IF I'M ON MY OWN.

YOU'RE BARELY WORTH MY TIME.
DID YOU REALLY BEAT MIDORIMA?

THE BRIGHTER THE LIGHT, THE STRONGER THE SHADOW.
SO DEPENDING ON HOW STRONG YOU SHINE, HE GETS STRONGER... OR WEAK-ER.

I FEEL SORRY FOR HIM NOW...
...CUZ HE'S A SHADOW.

OH, RIGHT. YOU'VE GOT TETSU TOO.
YOU ...!!
BAP

AND YOUR LIGHT...

...IS TOO DIM.

I'VE HAD ENOUGH OF THIS NON-SENSE.
SEE YA!

I'VE HAD MY TALK WITH TETSU-KUN.
IT'S TIME I HEAD BACK.

RIGHT. LET'S GET LUNCH AT SCHOOL.
THE AFTERNOON TRAINING STARTS AT ONE.

I PROMISE.
I'LL BEAT AOMINE-KUN.
MOMOI-SAN.

RIGHT...

HUH?
THAT YOU, SATSUKI?

HUH ?!
THAT'S MY LINE!
DON'T YOU HAVE PRAC-TICE TODAY ?!
YEAH.
WHY'RE YOU HERE TOO?
NOW PRACTICE IS ALMOST OVER.
AHHH, SO SLEEPY ...
WISH I HAD SOME RICE...
HEY...
TAKE IT DOWN A NOTCH.
AND I'M THE ONE WHO'S SAD, HERE.
THOUGHT I MIGHT FIND MYSELF SOME FUN, BUT IT WAS ALL A PIPE DREAM.
I MET THAT GUY, KAGAMI.
I'M ALWAYS TELLING YOU NOT TO SKIP!
BESIDES, HIS LEGS ARE PROBABLY STILL...

BAD LEGS OR NOT...
HE'S NOTHING.
TETSU MUST BE LOSING HIS EDGE.
CUZ THAT GUY...
...AIN'T CAPABLE OF DRAWING OUT TETSU'S POTENTIAL.

KUROKO'S BASKETBALL TAKE 2 BLOOPERS

AND YOUR LIGHT...
...IS TOO DIM.

I LOST...

HEY, DON'T HAVE TOO MANY COLD DRINKS JUST CUZ YOU'RE HOT.
IT'S ALMOST TIME FOR AFTER-NOON PRACTICE !!
RIGHT.

GAB
GAB
GAB

...BUT THIS WEIRD FEELING IS A FIRST FOR ME...
IT'S NOT LIKE IT'S THE FIRST TIME I LOST A ONE-ON-ONE... HECK, I ALSO LOST TO KISE THE FIRST TIME WE MET...

YEAHH !!
LET'S GO, SEIRIN!
EVERY-ONE'S GOTTA BELIEVE THAT WE'RE GOING TO INTER-HIGH!
SHK SHK
SHK
ALMOST TIME TO GET STARTED.
OKAY!
GOT IT!
SHK

...I COULDN'T WIN...
I FELT LIKE...

40TH QUARTER: DON'T MAKE ME LAUGH

CU
TE
TIME TO EAT.

...
CHOMP...
...

MUNCH
OH. LOOKS YUMMY.
YOINK
AH!

CUTE LUNCH YOU GOT THERE !!
HUH ?
MAYBE YOU GOT YOUR LITTLE SISTERS BY MISTAKE ?!
HUH? NO... I'M SORRY!
THERE'S NO MISTAKE, BECAUSE I MADE IT MYSELF...
MADE IT YOUR-SELF ?!

WHERE THE HELL WERE YOU EARLIER ?!
HM... AT A TEST ?
LIAR. THERE ARE NO TESTS TODAY!!
CHOMP
HEYA.
AOMINE !!

DON'T DO IT, SAKURAI !!
I'M SORRY! HERE YOU GO.
HUH ?
UH... WAIT, THIS IS...
SHOCK!
THIS STUFF'S GREAT. HAND IT OVER.
NOM NOM
I JUST FORGOT SOMETHING. HAD TO GO GET IT.
HA HA. SERIOUSLY?
YOU BETTER STICK AROUND FOR ALL OF AFTERNOON PRACTICE !!

I HAD A GOOD REASON, SO WHO CARES?
I'M TAKING OFF.
"LIAR"? "YOU BETTER"?
FREAKING ANNOYING.

POP...
I WENT OFF TO GET THIS PHOTO COLLECTION OF MAI HORIKITA.
MAI HORI-KITA
AND COMING BACK TO THE CLUBROOM WORE ME OUT.
I'M HEADING HOME.

SEE YOU GUYS.
WORK HARD!
OH!
YOU'RE GONNA START MAKING ME BENTO BOXES FROM NOW ON.
WHA-?!
ACK!
DECO-RATE THE FOOD WITH MAI-CHAN'S FACE.
OF COURSE. I'M SORRY!
WAIT, AOMINE !!

GIMME A BREAK THIS ONE TIME.
I'M JUST NOT FEELING IT TODAY.
AND GET OFFA ME.

KNOCK THIS CRAP OFF!
CHATTER
YOU GOTTA COME TO PRAC-TICES.
SHP

WHA...
WHAN
GAH!
AOMINE !!
I MEAN, I DID TELL HIM.
TO GET OFFA ME.
"PRACTICE, PRACTICE."
DON'T MAKE ME LAUGH.
RYO.
HOW MANY POINTS DID I SCORE LAST GAME?
UH...
82... POINTS.
YOU GUYS PRACTICE TO PREPARE FOR THE REAL THING, YEAH?
SO IF I SCORE POINTS, WHO CARES WHAT I DO IN THE MEAN-TIME?
BAP
BAP
IF YOU'RE GONNA NAG ME...
...THEN DO IT ONCE YOU'VE SHOWN...
SHK

KRAK
...ME...
SNAP
HUH ?
NOT AGAIN...
...
GUESS YOU'LL HAVE TO CANCEL TODAY'S PRACTICE ANYWAY.
UH... NOW WHERE WAS I...?
OH YEAH!

DO IT ONCE YOU'VE...
CLANG
CLATTER
...SHOWN ME UP.
BUT IT'S NEVER GONNA HAPPEN...

BECAUSE YOU WEREN'T WRONG...
...AND I COULDN'T SAY ANYTHING TO AOMINE.

SORRY, WAKA-MATSU.
WHY'RE YOU APOLO-GIZING, CAPTAIN ?!

CRAP...
GUH...
YOU OKAY ?!
SHK

HUH ?
OR HOW ABOUT ...
SHAQ ?
YOU MEAN SHAQUILLE O'NEAL...?

HE'S GOOD ENOUGH TO BE JUDGED SOLELY ON PERFORM-ANCE, WHICH IS RARE.
BUT...
JUST LIKE GOLF'S TIGER WOODS.
EVER HEARD OF HIM?

IN THE SPORTS WORLD, WHEN A SINGLE PLAYER IS JUST *THAT* GOOD...
...THEY CAN ACTUALLY END UP CHANGING THE RULES.
IT'S UN-COMMON ...
...BUT WE HAVE THE PERFECT EXAMPLE HERE...

BECAUSE TIGER WAS ABLE TO WIN WITH HIS CONSIS-TENTLY LONG DRIVES...
...COURSES GOT BIGGER. CLUBS ADAPTED NEW STANDARDS TO KEEP PLAYERS FROM HITTING OUT-OF-BOUNDS.
WITH SHAQ, HIS POWER MOVES WERE OFF THE CHARTS.
WE SAW A FLOOD OF DEFENDERS INTENTIONALLY DRAWING CHARGING FOULS FROM HIM, SO THE NO-CHARGE AREA WAS CREATED.

ANYHOW, IT'S NOT LIKE OUR TEAM...
...REALLY EVER RELIED ON TEAMWORK ALL THAT MUCH.
THAT MONSTER IS...
...CRAZY STRONG.
THE NEXT DAY...
EVERY-ONE!
THE LIST OF SCHOOLS IN THE FINALS LEAGUE...
...IS FINALLY HERE!!

SEIRIN
TO-OH ACADEMY
MEISEI
SEN-SHINKAN
SEIRIN
TO-OH ACADEMY
MEISEI
WE WON A-BLOCK, TO-OH ACADEMY WON B-BLOCK, MEISEI WON C-BLOCK AND SENSHINKAN WON D-BLOCK.
THESE FOUR TEAMS WILL BE BATTLING FOR SPOTS.

UP UNTIL LAST YEAR, IT WAS A SURE BET THAT YOU'D FIND TOKYO'S THREE KINGS IN HERE.
THIS LEAGUE LINEUP FEELS FRESH.
I KNOW MEISEI. THEY HAVE A GREAT PROGRAM.
TO-OH AND MEISEI... NEVER HEARD OF 'EM.

THEY'RE NOT AT SENSHINKAN...
THIS GUY...! HE'S JINXED US NOW!!
EVEN IF WE LOSE AGAINST MOMOI AND AOMINE, AS LONG AS WE BEAT THE OTHER TWO...
THIS YEAR... COULD WE REALLY GO ALL THE WAY ?!
I MEAN, WE ACTUALLY BEAT TWO OF THE KINGS.
I WAS THINKING...
FWASH

THOSE TWO GO TO...
...TO-OH ACADEMY.

WHAT ?!
I THOUGHT ALL THOSE MIRACLE GENERATION GUYS WENT TO TOP-NOTCH SCHOOLS.
LIKE HOW MIDORIMA WENT TO ONE OF THE KINGS...
I CHECKED OUT MOMOI'S UNIFORM AND DID SOME RESEARCH. I'M SURE OF IT.
I'VE NEVER HEARD OF THIS PLACE !!
HUHH
H?!

IT'S NOT A SCHOOL THAT'S ACHIEVED MUCH IN THE PAST...
...BUT LATELY, THEY'VE BEEN MAKING A REAL EFFORT AT SCOUTING.
TO-OH
ACADEMY
I HEAR THEY'RE RECRUITING PROMISING PLAYERS FROM AROUND THE COUNTRY.

THE PAST FEW YEARS'VE SEEN THEIR TEAM GROW IN ABILITY BY LEAPS AND BOUNDS.
THEIR LINEUP THIS YEAR MIGHT EVEN BE ON PAR WITH SHUTOKU'S.
同皇

NO WAY...
BUT...WHAT ABOUT SENSHIN-KAN?

YO!!
OH!
KAGA-MI!
YOU'RE LATE.

THEY'RE STRONG TOO, OF COURSE.
ANOTHER KING, JUST LIKE SEIHO AND SHUTOKU.
WE MIGHT'VE BEATEN THOSE TWO, BUT MAKE NO MISTAKE— WE'RE STILL A NOTCH BELOW THEM.
SO DON'T GET COCKY!

SHEESH...
HERE. A COPY OF THE LEAGUE LINEUP!
HOLD ON...
HUH?
MY BAD.
I WAS JUST CLEANING UP...

KLIK KLIK...
...

HOLD ON...
TWINGE
AND AGGRAVATING YOUR CONDITION...?
NO, OF COURSE N...
UH... NOPE.
HAVE YOU BEEN... PLAYING BASKETBALL?
KAGAMI-KUN...
91
8775
798

KRAK
YOU...
YOU KADUMMY !!
S-S-SORRY !!
GRAWR!
WAHHH!
WAHHH
YOU'RE SITTING OUT TODAY!!
GO GET A COMPRESS FROM THE NURSE'S OFFICE!!
OW!
ARE THOSE EARS OF YOURS JUST FOR DECORATION? ARE THEY JUST HOLES IN YOUR HEAD?!
...ALL THOSE TIMES!!
AFTER I TOLD YOU...
YIKES!
SHK...
EX-CUSE ME...
MAY I USE THE BATH-ROOM ?
SURE... JUST HURRY UP!
HUH ?!
FOR REAL ?!
START RUNNING!! OR RATHER, DON'T! WALK THERE ON YOUR HANDS!

KAGAMI-KUN...

...

I KNOW YOU'RE A FOOL, BUT...
HEY !!
I CAN'T IMAGINE YOU'D OVERDO IT FOR NO REASON.

FWIP
KURO-KO...
WHAT HAPPENED TO YOU?
WHOOPS!

I PLAYED ...
...AO-MINE.

!

WHO'S OUR FIRST GAME AGAINST ?
I'M UPSET BECAUSE KAGAMI-KUN IS SO INDISPENS-ABLE.
HE'S THE ONLY ONE WHO CAN MATCH UP AGAINST A MEMBER OF THE MIRACLE GENERATION...
GET WHAT I'M SAYING ?

OF ALL THE ...!
COME ON, COACH ...
BACK TO WHAT WE WERE SAY-ING.
HMPH!

OUR FIRST GAME IS AGAINST TO-OH ACADEMY !!
THE BIG ONE, RIGHT FROM THE START!

HE TOLD ME THAT...
...HE USED TO BE YOUR "LIGHT."
AND HE DIDN'T SEEM TO MEAN THAT IT WAS JUST CUZ YOU WERE ON THE SAME TEAM.

BACK IN MIDDLE SCHOOL...
WHAT HAPPENED TO YOU GUYS?

KUROKO'S BASKETBALL TAKE 2 BLOOPERS

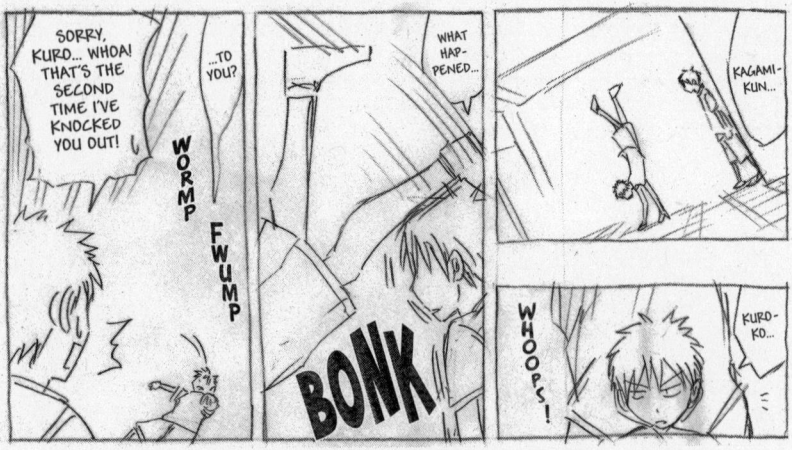

41ST QUARTER: IT'S "LEG," ACTUALLY

BACK IN MIDDLE SCHOOL...
WHAT HAPPENED TO YOU GUYS?

...

I'LL TELL YOU ON THE WAY BACK.
I CAN'T MISS OUT ON TOO MUCH PRACTICE...

BAP
SHK
SECOND YEAR OF MIDDLE SCHOOL, FIRST SUMMER...

AH...
K!!
SHUP
YOU KNOW WHAT, KISE?
CONSIDERING YOU ONLY JUST STARTED, THOSE ARE SOME NICE MOVES.
HA HA.
ONE MORE TIME! ONE MORE TIME!
C'MON!
IRK

I CAN'T BELIEVE HE'S ONLY A BEGINNER.
YEAH, GOING HEAD-TO-HEAD WITH OUR ACE, AOMINE.
SHK
SHK
KISE'S NOT BAD.
BAP
UH...
NAH... IT'S LIKE... HOW DO I PUT THIS?
AOMINE MUST RECOGNIZE THAT TALENT TOO. HE KEEPS PLAYING HIM, AFTER ALL...
GIVE HIM HALF A YEAR, AND I BET HE'LL TURN INTO A STAR PLAYER!
HE'S GOT THE HEIGHT TOO. AND HE KNOWS HOW TO HOLD ON TO THE BALL.
MM... SHOWS HE MUST HAVE SOME TALENT, RIGHT?
WHAT A KID!
WHAT THE HELL?
SIGH...
SURE, HE'S GOT THE MOST RAW TALENT. HE ALSO PRACTICES THE MOST ...
...BUT, MORE IMPORTANTLY...
THAT'S PROBABLY THE REAL REASON WHY HE'S OUR TEAM'S ACE.
HE JUST LIKES TO PLAY, I THINK...
AOMINE-KUN IS JUST A GYM RAT...

...MORE THAN ANYONE ELSE...
...HE JUST LOVES BASKET-BALL.

SURE... IT'S GREAT HOW AWESOME HE IS AT B-BALL.
BUT HOW DID HE GET TO BE FRIENDS WITH YOU WHEN YOU WERE KIDS?
I WISH I HAD A CUTIE AS A GIRL-FRIEND TOO.
I'M NOT HIS GIRL-FRIEND !!
WE'RE JUST LINKED, WHETHER I LIKE IT OR NOT.

IT'S NOT AS THOUGH...
...MIDORIMA-KUN AND KISE-KUN WERE BEASTS FROM THE START.
...
THOSE GUYS IN THE SO-CALLED MIRACLE GENERA-TION...
...WERE JUST ABOVE-AVERAGE PLAYERS DURING THEIR FIRST AND SECOND YEARS OF MIDDLE SCHOOL.
THAT'S ALL.
BUT AOMINE-KUN WAS THE FIRST...
...TO REALLY BLOSSOM.
AND IT HAPPENED SUDDENLY.

SHU
P!!
光
6
AOMINE'S AMAZING!! HE'S IN TOP FORM!!
HE'S CRUSHING THEM ALL ON HIS OWN.
NOBODY CAN STOP THAT GUY!!
YEAH
HU

INCREDIBLE !!
帝光
6
I ALWAYS KNEW AOMINE WAS GOOD...
BUT THIS GOOD ...?
THAT MAKES FIFTY POINTS FOR THIS GAME...
HE'S LIKE A WHOLE NEW PERSON ...
ALMOST ... TOO GOOD ...
BZZZZZZ...
TEIKO
0:00
YOSEN
173
51

YONEYA
31
0:00
TEIKO
203

HERE.
STEEL YOUNG WINNER

YEAH, WHAT-EVER.
MORE PRACTICE MEANS YOU GET BETTER, I GET IT.

AOMINE-KUN...
YOU'VE BEEN SKIPPING OUT ON MORE AND MORE PRACTICES LATELY.

BUT THE HARDER I TRY...
...THE MORE BORING BASKETBALL GETS.
BE-SIDES, I KNOW ...
...THE ONE I'M LOOKING FOR JUST ISN'T...

AOMINE-CHI'S GOTTEN CRAZY GOOD LATELY, HUH?
BASKET-BALL MUST BE TONS OF FUN FOR HIM AT THIS POINT!
...
NO. RATHER ...
...THE OPPOSITE, I SUSPECT.
HUH ?
WHY'S THAT?
BECAUSE HE LOVES BASKETBALL MORE THAN ANY OF US...
...THERE'S SOMETHING HE SEEKS ABOVE ALL ELSE.
SOMEONE WHO CAN FACE HIM HEAD-ON...
A RIVAL.
HE'S ALWAYS BEEN GOOD, OF COURSE ...
...BUT ONLY A BIT BETTER THAN THE REST OF US.
HE'S TOO GOOD NOW, THOUGH.
FORGET FINDING A RIVAL. THE GULF BETWEEN HIM AND ALL THE OTHERS IS ONLY OPENING WIDER.
OVER-WHELM-INGLY SO.

BASKET-BALL HAS BECOME NOTHING BUT A GAME TO ME.
I'LL JUST LET OUR GAMES PLAY OUT FROM NOW ON...

YOU CAN'T DO THAT.
SHF
HYAH!
WHAT THE—?!
YOUR POPSICLE ?!

I ALWAYS TRY MY HARDEST BECAUSE OTHER-WISE I'LL LAG BEHIND...
I CAN'T BEGIN TO EVEN UNDERSTAND YOUR FEELINGS.
BUT...

NO MATTER HOW GREAT THE DIFFER-ENCE IN SKILL...
...I WOULD NEVER, EVER WANT...
...AN OPPONENT WHO...
...HOLDS BACK OR JUST STANDS ASIDE.

YOU JERK!
HA HA.
I'M SURE SOMEONE BETTER THAN YOU WILL SHOW UP SOON.
BE-SIDES ...
YOU'RE RIGHT.
BUMP
I KNOW.
YEAH
H
HH

HE HAS THIS REALLY GOOD FOCUS ABOUT HIM.
WEIRD.
TODAY... AOMINE-KUN HAS...
WHOOAAA
NICE! THAT'S FORTY POINTS FROM HIM.
HE'S INCRED-IBLE.

HE'S DOMINATING!
EVEN UP AGAINST THE LEADING MIDDLE SCHOOL FORWARD, INOUE-KUN, WHO'S GIVEN HIM TROUBLE COUNTLESS TIMES...

BAP
SHD
YEAH!!
SHK!!
FWIP

HUH?
...

...BUT LOOK AT THEM.
IT'S LIKE THEY'VE LOST ALL THEIR FIGHT.

TEIKO
KAMIZAKI
I UNDERSTAND IT'S HARD FOR THEM TO STAY MOTIVATED ...
THAT LARGE LEAD IS THE RESULT OF AOMINE GETTING SERIOUS

I CAN MAKE THE OPPONENT GIVE UP ALL HOPE.
HA HA. SO THIS IS HOW IT GOES WHEN I PLAY MY HEART OUT?

HOW'S THIS S'POSED TO BE FUN FOR ME?

BUT... IT'S NOT WORKING.
I'M NOT SAYING YOU WERE WRONG ABOUT ALL THAT STUFF.

SHK...
TETSU ...

...THAT WHAT I'M LOOKING FOR ISN'T OUT THERE.
NO ONE CAN POSSIBLY MEASURE UP TO ME.
ALL THESE KIDS... THEY'RE WORTH-LESS.
I'M REALIZING NOW...

THE ONLY ONE WHO CAN BEAT ME...
...IS ME.
HMPH...
IF I COULD TELL THAT GUY ONE THING, IT'D BE ...
...I QUIT THE TEIKO BASKET-BALL CLUB IN MY THIRD YEAR.
AND BECAUSE OF SOMETHING THAT HAPPENED DURING NATIONALS...
WE CRUSHED THE MIDDLE SCHOOL NATIONALS THAT SUMMER THANKS TO AOMINE-KUN.
BUT THAT'S WHEN THE OTHER FOUR ALSO BEGAN TO CHANGE ...

GET THE HELL OFF YOUR HIGH HORSE, MORON!
OR SOME-THING LIKE THAT.

GIMME YOUR HAND...
HUH?
JUST DO IT.
NO. NOT FOR A HAND-SHAKE. A FIST!

HE'S SO GOOD IT GOT BORING ?
WHO KNEW THE MIRACLE GENERA-TION HAD AN IDIOT LIKE THAT!

YOU GOTTA BE PULLING MY ARM.
IT'S "LEG," ACTU-ALLY.

THE ONLY ONE WHO CAN BEAT HIM IS HIM?

LET'S BEAT HIM GOOD...
BUMP...
...AND SHOW HIM WHAT A MORON HE IS.

BE-
FORE
LONG
...
...IT
WAS
TIME
FOR
THE
DECI-
SIVE
GAME.

KUROKO'S BASKETBALL TAKE 18 BLOOPERS

42ND QUARTER: OPENING ACT

CHIRP
CHIRP
CHIRP...

FSSH
H....

7:23
MONTH DATE
6/23 FRI
BAT

CHK
I'LL BEAT AOMINE-KUN.
I PROMISE.

TMP
TMP
TMP...

PHEW...
FINALLY TIME...

IT STARTS TODAY, RIGHT? HOW WONDER-FUL.
HUH?
TMP
TMP
THE FINALS LEAGUE ...

MOM...
HMPH...
I CRACK MYSELF UP. HEH HEH!!
AND HERE'S YOUR OOLONG TO GET THE PAR...TEA STARTED!
I'LL BE CHEERING YOU ON!

THAT DE-LICIOUS PUN.
PING
I'LL TAKE IT...
...TO GO!!
GAB
GAB
GAB
YOU'VE GOTTA HEAD OUT SOON...
IT'S FINE, BIG BRO. YOU EAT.
WAHHH!
YIKES!
HEY... THAT'S MY EGG!!
AHHHH!
OH?! WE'RE OUT OF SAUSAGE?
THERE'S PLENTY OF MISO SOUP. TAKE THAT INSTEAD!!
YAP
YAP
SLAP
A LITTLE LONGER... THE GAME'S NOT UNTIL NIGHT... NIGHT...
UGHHH...
YOU'RE GONNA BE LATE, SILLY!
BRUSH
BRUSH
AND YOU'VE GOT SCHOOL UNTIL THEN!!
BAKIMAN

SHOCK!!
HEY. IT'S MORNING. YOU GOING TO SCHOOL...?
YOU SURE ARE ENTHUSI-ASTIC.

COME ON... AT LEAST KNOCK, DAD!
DID YOU STAY UP ALL NIGHT?
THAT'S NOT GOOD FOR YOUR LOOKS, YOU KNOW!!
TODAY'S OPPONENT IS UNREAL...
THAT'S WHY I'M AT IT LIKE THIS.
YAWN...

I GUESS I'M A LITTLE TIRED...
A QUICK SHOWER SHOULD WAKE ME UP.
HEY, RIKO!
YOU LEFT YOUR PANTIES LYING AROUND !!
GET THE HELL OUTTA HERE, YOU PERV!!
KAPOW!

OKAY... I DIDN'T FORGET ANYTHING! I'M OFF.
HM?
MEW
HERE. HERE.
PRETTY KITTY.
CHOMP
YEE...
...OWCH !!
SWISH...
TCH...
GET READY FOR A RUDE AWAKENING, AOMINE...
NICE! NO MORE PAIN!!

SHP
I'M GONNA WIN!!
TTMP...
TTMP...
TTMP...

CHATTER...
CHATTER...
MUTTER...

WHOA, WHOA.
I SHOULD HAVE KNOWN THE FINALS LEAGUE WOULD ATTRACT A CROWD LIKE THIS.

THERE'S REALLY ONLY ONE GAME WORTH WATCHING TODAY.
OUT OF C- AND D-BLOCK'S WINNERS, SENSHINKAN AND MEISEI...
WE KNOW SENSHIN-KAN'S GONNA WIN.

SEEMS LIKE HE'S NOT COMING ...
HA HA. I'LL MURDER HIM.
SORRY. MY FAMILY'S PICKUP IS BROKEN DOWN.
HIS TEXT JUST SAYS, "I DON'T WANT TO"...
I'LL KILL HIM ANOTHER WAY...

STOP WANDERING AROUND, TAKAO.
HEH.
HUH? WHERE'S MIDORIMA ?

MEISEI'S NOT A BAD TEAM, BUT NOWHERE NEAR ELITE.
WHAT'S GONNA DETERMINE THE FINALS LEAGUE IS SEIRIN VERSUS TO-OH ACADEMY!

HUH ?!
AOMINE-KUN'S STILL NOT HERE ?!

AND HE WON'T ANSWER MY CALLS.
THAT JERK...
SORRY, SORRY. IT'S ALL BECAUSE I'M SO WORTH-LESS...
FWIP
HOLD ON... LEMME TRY!!

BEEP BEEP BEEP
RING...
RING...
CLICK
YO.
HE PICKED UP!!
WHAT'RE YOU DOING?! WHERE ARE YOU?!
THE GAME'S ABOUT TO START!!
WHAT'M I...? I'M AT SCHOOL ...

OH...
SORRY.
YAWN...
OVER-SLEPT.
OVER-SLEPT?! AOMINE! HOW QUICK CAN YOU GET HERE?!
OH! THAT YOU, IMAYOSHI-SAN?
HM...
PROBABLY... BY THE SECOND HALF...
PLEASE DO SO!! WE'RE UP AGAINST THAT SEIRIN SCHOOL!
HA HA.
THAT ALL?
TWENTY MINUTES IS MORE THAN ENOUGH TIME TO CRUSH NOBODIES LIKE THEM.
SO...
JUST HANG IN THERE IN THE FIRST HALF.
HUH? HEY...
KLIK

WE'LL START WITH JUST US...
...AND DO WHAT WE CAN.
IT IS WHAT IT IS.
WHAT A DRAG...
I'M SORRY... ABOUT THAT IDIOT...
IT'S ALMOST TIME...
EVERY-ONE...
ARE YOU READY FOR THIS?!

THIS FIRST MATCH IS CRITICAL!!
AS YOU ALL WELL KNOW, ONLY THREE OF FOUR TEAMS MOVE ON TO INTER-HIGH!
LIKE KOGANEI-KUN, SOME OF YOU MIGHT THINK THERE'S NOTHING TO WORRY ABOUT, BUT...

HM ...?!
SHP
HUH?! WHAT ?!
HOLD ON. MITO... IZUKI ?!
SHP

DON'T GET COCKY !!
BWAHH!
SLAP

YOU MIGHT BE TEMPTED TO THINK THAT GIVEN THE FINALS LEAGUE FORMAT...
...THAT ONE LOSS IS FINE. BUT THAT'S HOW YOU END UP LOSING IT ALL.
WHYYY?!
WHY'D I GET SLAPPED ?!
!?
AND I'M THE ONE WHO MADE THAT PAPER-FAN SLAPPER IN THE FIRST PLACE.
THIS GAME MEANS EVERY-THING!!

"I'LL TRY HARDER NEXT TIME" ISN'T REAL DETERMINATION. IT'S AN EXCUSE!
CUZ YOU'LL JUST FAIL THE NEXT TIME TOO!
YOU GOTTA WIN THIS !!
SEIRIN HIGH SCHOOL LOCKER ROOM
3
LET'S GO...
SEIRIN !!
YEAHHH !!

CHATTER...
RAWRR
RRR...
IT'S SEIRIN ...
OOH, HERE THEY COME !!
...AND TO-OH ACAD-EMY!!
HE'S LATE.
THE SELFISH JERK.
SHK
UM...
WHERE'S AOMINE?
I DON'T SEE HIM.
HUH ?
SHK
SHK
...?!

WHA ...?!
...?!
I'M SORRY.
WE'RE NOT HAPPY ABOUT HIS ABSENCE EITHER...

HE SAID HE'D COME FOR THE SECOND HALF.
WHICH KIND OF MAKES US SEEM LIKE... THE OPENING ACT.
SO GO EASY ON US, OKAY?

GO EASY ON THEM? SERIOUSLY ...?
WEIRD.

...THE MATCH ...
...BE-TWEEN ...
...SEIRIN HIGH SCHOOL ...
...AND TO-OH ACADEMY.
WE WILL SOON BEGIN...

GET READY!

SHK...
KAGAMI.
I HEARD YOU ALREADY HAD A CHANCE TO MEET AOMINE.
I HOPE YOU'RE NOT LACKING IN THE MOTIVATION DEPARTMENT...
...JUST BECAUSE HE'S NOT HERE.
NO WAY.

I'M MAD AS HELL...

...SIR.

OPENING ACT? *HAH!* I'LL BURY 'EM SO DEEP THAT NOT EVEN *HE'LL* BE ABLE TO BRING THEM BACK.

HE'LL BE THE BIGGEST LAUGHING-STOCK THERE EVER WAS.

BUT THERE'S NO SENSE IN GETTING ANGRY AT SOMEONE WHO'S NOT HERE.

THE OPPONENT IN FRONT OF US IS ALL THERE IS.

RAWR
GO ALL OUT !!
SHUP!!
R
R
IT'S START-ED!!
SHOOF
TCH!

WHO
!!
OSH
HE'S QUICK !!
...!!

...IN ORDER TO DO THAT....
...WE'VE GOTTA STOP HIM AND TAKE CONTROL OF THE GAME!!
IF THIS REALLY IS OUR CHANCE TO PULL AHEAD, THEN...

NO MATTER.
IN THAT CASE...
QUICK TO RESPOND, I SEE.

4

SHp
...WE'LL LET OUR SPECIAL SHOOTER BOMB AWAY.
SHK
TO START THINGS OFF...
CHF...
6
!

I'M SORRY !!
FWISH!!
相皇
GAKUEN
9
KTUNK
SH
A THREE-POINTER !!
ARGH!
BUT THE WAY HE MOVES IS ALL OVER THE PLACE...!
SO FAST !!
HE APOLOGIZED?

...STRONG !!
THEY'RE JUST THAT...
IT'S NOT LIKE WE GOT CARELESS OR ANYTHING...
IT'S NOT JUST #9... THE OTHER FOUR TOO...
WE'RE NOTHING COMPARED TO HIM.
YOU'LL UNDERSTAND ONCE AOMINE'S HERE.
...!!
HUH?
IT WASN'T A LIE AT ALL.
THAT WAS DIRTY, LYING ABOUT BEING THE OPENING ACT.
SO AS I SAID...
ENJOY THIS OPENING ACT.

KUROKO'S BASKETBALL BLOOPERS

TAKE 9

43RD QUARTER: I GOT IT

WHY DO YOU ALWAYS GOTTA SHOUT SOMETHING WEIRD?
"EAT THIS" ?
SHUP
GOTTA STOP HIM!
SHK
SHUP
...THIS !!
SHK
SWIP!
WHAT A PASS...!!

FLIP...
FWISH!
WHEN I SAID "OPENING ACT"...
...I MEANT IN COMPARISON TO AOMINE.
WELL, I'M SORRY. MAYBE I PHRASED IT POORLY.
WHEN YOU HEARD THAT OUR ACE, AOMINE, WAS LATE, YOU WERE PROBABLY THINKING YOU'D TAKE THE INITIATIVE...
RA
WR
WOW!
DOUBLE CLUTCH?!
SWISH

43RD QUARTER: I GOT IT

YEAHHH
AND THIS IS JUST THE BEGINNING... I CAN'T IMAGINE HOW IT'LL BE WHEN AOMINE-KUN DOES SHOW UP.
SO STRONG ...!
YEAH
WOW. TRIPLE DIGITS EVERY TIME?!
108 TO 91.
151 TO 72.
131 TO 81.
AKANISHI
AO
TO-OH ACADEMY
WHAT'D YOU NOTICE ?
WHOAA?! IT MAKES SENSE NOW.
TO-OH'S SCORES THROUGHOUT THE QUALIFIER TOURNAMENT.
YEAH
YEAH!
A PURELY OFFENSIVE TEAM.
YEP.
THEY'RE THE EXACT OPPOSITE OF SEIHO...

DAMN. SO HARD TO BLOCK!! HE SHOOTS WHILE HE JUMPS...!!
AND IF YOU'RE GONNA APOLOGIZE, THEN DON'T SHOOT AT ALL!
SHUP
FWISH
I'M SORRY!
TAP
CLANG
AND THESE GUYS...
GAH!
CHP...
OHHH!
I'M SORRY!!
EEK!
BUMP

BOTH OFFENSE AND DEFENSE ARE ALWAYS ONE-ON-ONE.
THEY'RE NOT MAKING THE SLIGHTEST ATTEMPT TO HELP EACH OTHER OR WORK AS A TEAM.

THESE GUYS ...

ALL THEIR FOCUS IS ON INDIVIDUAL TECHNIQUES!
IF ONE OF THEM GETS THE BALL, IT'S UP TO HIM TO SINK IT...

OUR TEAM'S MADE UP OF NATIONAL-LEVEL CHAMPS.
EACH IS A FORCE TO BE RECKONED WITH. THAT'S OUR SELLING POINT.
WE'VE EXPERI-MENTED OVER THE YEARS, BUT...

OH?

I GET IT.
TO SOME EXTENT, I HAD AN INKLING THIS IS HOW IT'D TURN OUT...
...WITH YOUR TEAM'S STYLE...
SHK...

YEAHHH
RATHER THAN JOINING HANDS AND COOPERATING...
...WE FIND THAT *THIS* WAY WORKS WAY BETTER.
桐皇
GAKUEN
YEAH
INTERESTING OR NOT...
WE'RE DEFINITELY NOT THE SAME.
YOURS IS A TEAM ALSO BUILT ON OFFENSE.
THIS SHOULD BE INTERESTING.
桐皇
GAKUEN
YEAHH
BECAUSE OUR STYLE...
...IS TO ATTACK AS ONE.
YEAHH

S...K!
UGH...
BAP
桐皇
GAKUEN
4
5

SHK
SHK
?!
BAP
NOT SO FAST !!
5

ONE-ON-ONE MATCHES ARE ONE THING.
SHUP
SHK
TURN
SHK
9
8

BUT WE DON'T PLAN ON LOSING THIS GAME.
TELL YOUR CAPTAIN THAT, LI'L MR. SORRY.
SWISH!
HUH?! I'M SORRY!
LI'L MR. SORRY ?!
I DIDN'T EVEN SAY ANYTHING!
SHOCK!
HA HA HA!
I COULDN'T QUITE HEAR THAT, BUT YOUR PLAY SAID IT ALL, LOUD AND CLEAR...

FWIP!
HAH!!
FLING
WELL... REMEMBER HOW I SAID WE PLAY AS ONE?
OUR STYLE OR YOUR STYLE...
LET'S SEE WHICH IS BETTER.
WHA...?! ANOTHER LONG PASS?!
WE'VE GOT ONE GUY WHO PEOPLE ALWAYS SEEM TO FORGET.
SHK
WAIT, ISN'T THAT GUY LEADING THE BREAK SUPPOSED TO BE THE CENTER?!
SO QUICK!
RAWR

桐皇
GAKUEN
SEIRIN
11

WHERE THE HECK DID YOU COME FROM?!
BUT... HOW COULD HE—?!
FAST !!
SHUP!
SO SHORT, THOUGH !!
SHOCK
SHEESH ...
STICK TO WHAT YOU'RE GOOD AT, IDIOT!

HU

S
SO HIGH!
IT'S TOO HIGH. CRAZY HIGH. WHAT A JUMP... WHO THE HECK IS THIS GUY ?!

BUMP
SORRY!
SLAM

FWIP...
NICE, KAGAMI!
AND, KUROKO ...?

WHAT'S WITH THAT LAME JUMP?
IF YOU CAN'T GET IT, DON'T TRY!
I HAD IT.
LIAR !!
SHK
SHK...
THAT WASN'T LIKE YOU.
ARE YOU STILL FEELING HUNG UP ON THAT OLD SCHOOL OF YOURS?

YEAHH
LIAR!!
BUT... I HAD IT.
SNAP OUT OF IT!
WE'RE FACING TO-OH ACADEMY NOW.
HM... IT'S JUST LIKE THEY SAY.
YEAHH
YEAHH
THAT JERK MADE A FOOL OUTTA ME!
UH...
SHK
HM?
AND THEY'RE LOSING AGAIN...
YEAHH
YEAH
DARN...
I'M LATE AGAIN.
YEA

MIDORIMA-CHI?!
WAIT... WHO'RE YOU SUPPOSED TO BE?
HUH?
KISE?! HOW'D YOU KNOW IT WAS ME?!
THEY'RE JUST SUN-GLASSES, DUMMY!
AND DOWNRIGHT EMBAR-RASSING, AT THAT. TAKE 'EM OFF!
GASP!
AND WHAT THE HECK'S THAT THING?
WHA—?!

INTERESTING. YOU TELL EVERYONE YOU DON'T WANNA WATCH, BUT NOW I FIND YOU HERE ANYWAY?
THIS IS TODAY'S LUCKY ITEM, OF COURSE.
WHY THE INTERROGATION? I JUST HAPPENED TO BE PASSING THROUGH THE AREA. THAT'S ALL!
BUT YOUR HOUSE IS THE OTHER WAY.
ZING

YEAHHH
ANYWAY, HOW'S THE GAME GOING?
HARDLY WORTH OUR TIME...
YEAHHHHH
DIS-GRACEFUL, IN FACT.
AOMINE'S NOT EVEN HERE...
...AND THEY'RE STILL STRUG-GLING TO KEEP UP.
AOMINE-CHI'S NOT HERE?!

YEAHHH
HAVE YOU FORGOTTEN, KISE?
YEAHHH
IT ALL STARTS NOW.
BUT, HEY, THOSE TWO ARE JUST GETTING WARMED UP.

!
TO-OH HAS MOMOI ON THEIR SIDE.

SO, THIS TIME AROUND ...
SHE SAVED OUR SKINS TIME AFTER TIME IN MIDDLE SCHOOL.
AND SHE'S NO ORDINARY MANAGER.
YEAHHH

...THEY COULDN'T HAVE ASKED...
...FOR A DEADLIER ENEMY.

KUROKO'S BASKETBALL BLOOPERS

TAKE 1

SHONEN JUMP MANGA
6
ONE THING I WON'T DO!!
Kuroko's
BASKETBALL
TADATOSHI FUJIMAKI

TADATOSHI FUJIMAKI

This isn't something I typically broadcast, but I often find myself irritated while working, thinking, "Why can't I draw better?" or "Why can't I come up with a better story?" But I believe that satisfaction means the end of passion, so I'll probably keep being irritated.

But I like drawing manga.

—2010

44TH QUARTER: NOT HER STYLE

44TH QUARTER: NOT HER STYLE

YEAHHH
MAIN EXIT
GOTTA SAY, SHE'S A CUTIE.
SO I HEARD THAT CHICK'S YOUR EX.
YEAHHH
OH. YOU THINK SO?
HEY!
YER REALLY STARTING TO BUG ME!
WELL, I SUPPOSE SHE IS...
HUH ?!
YEAHHH
YEAHH
AT LEAST OFF THE COURT...
YEAHHH

YEAHHH

RUB

RUB

I CAN SEE HOW THESE GUYS TOPPLED THE KINGS.

To-oh Academy Coach
KATSUNORI HARASAWA

YEAHH

YES.

BESIDES, MOMOI-SAN HAS ALREADY PROVIDED THEM WITH WHAT THEY NEED.

OUR BOYS'LL FIGURE IT OUT ONCE THEY KNOW WHAT THEY'RE UP AGAINST.

NAH, IT'S FINE.

COACH... SHOULDN'T WE CALL A TIME-OUT?

YEAHHH

...EVERY-THING.

WE KNOW...

YEAHHH

SHP
!!
THEY'RE LEAVING THE PERIMETER OPEN, SO I CAN'T GET INSIDE...
THESE JERKS... THEIR DEFENSE IS PRETTY STIFF...
SHP
SHK
TOMP TOMP TOMP TOMP TOMP
OOH, NICE STEAL !!
DASH
A THREE-POINTER ?! NO...
SHUP
SUCK-ERS !!
FWISH
...AN ALLEY-OOP!!
HE'S THROW-ING HIM-SELF ...

KNEW IT. ♡
I SAW THIS COMING.
SHK
IT'S SO LIKE A BOY TO TRY SOME-THING SO SIMPLE.
GAKUEN
SHUMP

KLANK
FWUMP
GRK
THEIR MOVEMENT... IT'S LIKE THEY'VE SEEN ME TRY THAT BEFORE!!
YEAHHH
SHUP
NOW THEY KNOW KAGAMI'S NOT A GREAT OUTSIDE SHOOTER.
WHICH MEANS...
YEAHHH

YEAHHH
SOME-ONE'S BEEN STUDYING UP ON US.
PROBABLY MOMOI.
YEAHHH
MOMOI'S TRUE ROLE? SHE'S AN INTEL-GATHERING SCOUT.
LIKE A SECRET AGENT, BASICALLY.
GO, MITOBE !!
YEAHHH
FWIP
SHK
YEAHH
RA
W
R

SLAP
SHUP
A HOOK SHOT, RIGHT?!
WE CAN SMELL YOUR CRAP FROM A MILE AWAY!!
THIS IS BAD!! WE NEED A STRATEGY HERE...
NO, WE DON'T!
THEY READ HIM LIKE A BOOK!!
STAY THE COURSE!
YEAHHH
YEAHHH

YEAHHH
PEOPLE GROW AND CHANGE.
ALL THAT INFO IS FROM THE PAST.
IT DOESN'T MATTER HOW ACCURATE THEIR INTEL IS...
HUH ?!
YEAHH!

...ALL THEIR KNOWLEDGE IS FOR NOTHING!
WITHOUT THAT BIT OF COMMON SENSE...
YEAHH!

HYUGA'S GOING FOR A THREE!!

...!!

FWIP
9

YEAHHH
HYUGA'S A PURE SHOOTER.
WE GOT 'EM!!
NICE!

...WORKING ON HIS DRIBBLING SKILLS.
THAT'S WHY HE'S BEEN TRAINING LIKE MAD SINCE OUR GAME AGAINST SHUTOKU ...

BUT...
IN RECENT YEARS, LONG-RANGE SHOOTERS'VE FOUND THEMSELVES OUTMATCHED.

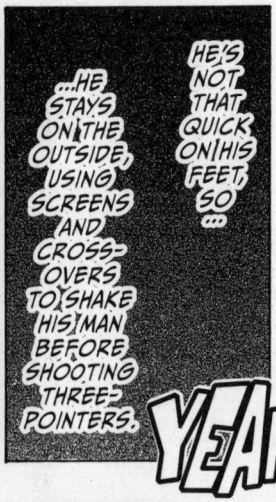
HE'S NOT THAT QUICK ON HIS FEET, SO ...
...HE STAYS ON THE OUTSIDE, USING SCREENS AND CROSS-OVERS TO SHAKE HIS MAN BEFORE SHOOTING THREE-POINTERS.
YEAH!

IF THE OPPONENT'S CONVINCED HE'S JUST GONNA SHOOT, THEN...
...HE CAN BREAK FREE !!
FWOOP

I CAN'T EXACTLY SAY HE'S FAST, BUT...
...IF HE TRIES THIS NEW PLAY...
...WHEN THEY'RE EXPECTING NOTHING BUT THREE-POINTERS ...
YEAHHH

HK
SEIRIN
4
KNEW IT. ♡
I EXPECTED HIM TO CHANGE IT UP THAT WAY.

GUH ...?!
!!
THEY SHOULDN'T HAVE ANY REPORTS ON IT!
BUT THEY'VE NEVER SEEN THIS MOVE BEFORE ...
NORMALLY, ONE WOULDN'T BE ABLE TO REACT TO A NEW AND UNKNOWN STRATEGY...
BUT MOMOI ACTUALLY ANALYZES THE DATA SHE COLLECTS.
THAT LETS HER PREDICT HOW THE OPPONENT WILL EVOLVE.
A PLAYER'S HEIGHT, WEIGHT, STRENGTHS, WEAKNESSES, PERSONALITY, HABITS.
I ANALYZE IT ALL TO MAKE CONCLUSIONS...
AND MY FINAL SECRET ...?

A WOMAN'S INTUITION. ♡

SHK
TCH...
BAP

...

MOVE IT BACK, HYUGA!
FWIP

5
HE'S ONLY GOT FIVE SECONDS !!

WE CAN'T SEEM TO ATTACK ...!!
NO GOOD. THEY'RE READING OUR EVERY MOVE...

I THOUGHT YOU MIGHT GO THAT FAR, ACTUALLY.
DON'T UNDER-ESTIMATE US, SWEETIE!
GRIN
FWIP
SHK
SHK
BAP
THERE'S ANOTHER REASON I SAID WE SHOULD STAY THE COURSE.
A SIMPLE ONE... THAT IS...
YEAHHH
THUMP
...?!
SAME AS BEFORE. HE CAN'T MAKE IT PAST !!
YEAHHH

BECAUSE EVEN A WOMAN'S INTUITION...
A WOMAN'S INTUITION!

...CAN'T PREDICT WHAT HE'LL DO NEXT!
A SCREEN ?!
WHAT ?!
HUH ?!
MY MAN VANISHED INTO THIN AIR!!

TO-OH ACADEMY
2:15
SEIRIN
21
15
SEIRIN
1
KA
KASA
YEAH
GOOD WORK OUT THERE AS ALWAYS, KUROKO!
NICE ONE, KAGAMI !!
SHK
SHK

YEAHHH
THERE'S NO READING HIM. SAME AS EVER.
IT'S FINE.
GAHHH! I SHOULD'VE KNOWN THIS WOULDN'T BE SO SIMPLE.
YEAHHH
SHEESH...
11
YEAHHH
...THAT'S WHY...
...I LIKE TETSU-KUN!
BUT...
BECAUSE I EVEN SAW THIS COMING.
...?!
SHK
GOTTA HOLD THEM!!
DEFENSE, NOW!
!
TWINGE

KUROKO'S BASKETBALL BLOOPERS

TAKE 10

45TH QUARTER: LET'S DO THIS!

BZZZZZ
THE FIRST QUARTER IS OVER.
TO-OH ACADEMY
1:58
SEIRIN
25
21

HAHH
HAHH
WOW...
HAHH
YEAHHH
PFFT. MOMOI'S DATA GIVES US ALL WE NEED TO WIN THIS.
AOMINE DOESN'T EVEN NEED TO SHOW UP!
YEAHHH
A FOUR-POINT GAP...
WELL...
THAT'S JUST HOW IT IS.
YEAHHH
OR DO I REALLY HAVE TO STATE THE OBVIOUS AND TELL YOU ALL TO NOT GET CARELESS?
NO. I AM GOING TO PLAY HIM.
YEAHHH
YES...
WITHOUT A DOUBT...
YEAHH
STARTING IN THE SECOND QUARTER ...
...I'M THINKING THOSE TWO WILL BE WORKING THE COURT.

YEAHHH
YEAHHH
...AND ATTACK!
KUROKO-KUN AND KAGAMI-KUN WILL TAKE THE LEAD...
SEIRIN
4
15
YEAHHH
HUH ?
WE'RE REALLY LUCKY TO HAVE THESE TWO NEWBIES.
YEAHHH
RIGHT.
WE'RE COUNTING ON YOU GUYS.
SHK
BUT WITH YOU TWO, THERE'S MUCH LESS TO WORK WITH.
KUROKO-KUN'S TOUGH TO PREDICT, AND KAGAMI-KUN'S AN UP-AND-COMER.
IF THERE'S ANYONE WHO COULD CHALLENGE MOMOI, IT'D BE YOU TWO.
THE MORE DATA YOU'VE GOT, THE BIGGER THE ADVANTAGE.
HYUGA-KUN AND THE OTHER SECOND-YEARS HAVE GIVEN HER A WHOLE YEAR'S WORTH OF INTEL.
YEAHHH

THE LEASH IS OFF, ROOKIES!
BZZZZZZ
YEAHHH
SHK
SHK
YEAHH
...!!
LET'S MAKE THIS HAPPEN!
GOOD.
SHK
!!!
MWA HA HA! RIGHT OFF THE BAT, HUH?
FWEE
SHK

HH!
SEIRIN
10
GAKUEN
7
11

IT'S TRUE OUR DATA ON THESE TWO IS PRETTY LIMITED...
SHUP
AHHH!
THIS CRAP MIGHT'VE WORKED IN MIDDLE SCHOOL, KID...
ISN'T THIS THE PLAY THAT FAILED AGAINST SHUTOKU?!
UKK
...BUT YOUR STUPID DUNKS WON'T CUT IT HERE!!
THOSE TWO'RE BLOCKING HIM!!
RAWR
...!!
WHAT THE HELL ...?!
HOW HIGH CAN HE GET ...?

SLAM
THROB

THOSE UPS... HIS SKILLS ARE NO FREAKING JOKE!!
EVEN THOUGH WE KNEW IN ADVANCE...
DAMN!
IS HE UN-STOP-PABLE...?!
HAHH
HAHH
I'LL KICK YOU ALL TO THE CURB...
AND JUMP RIGHT OVER YOU!
YEAHHH
STILL, NICE ONE, KADUMMY!!
IS DUNKING ALL YOU CAN DO?
SMACK
I SCORED. GIMME A BREAK!!
SMACK
...IF YOU PUNKS ARE TOO SLOW TO KEEP UP!
ALL THE DATA IN THE WORLD WON'T HELP...
...
SHK

YEAHHH
GO! GO, KAGAMI!!
HAHH
HAHH
YEAHHH
WHOA, KAGAMI'S ON A ROLL!
TWO IN A ROW !!
GO, GO!!
YEAHHH

HE'S IN BAD SHAPE.
NO...

YOUTH ONLY GOES SO FAR...
...AND EVERY BODY HAS ITS BREAKING POINT.
HE'S DONE.

THIS IS AN EMERGENCY.
QUICK, GET IN, KOGANEI-KUN!

...?!
KLIK...
OH NO ...!!

SEIRIN MAKES A SUBSTITUTION.
BZZZZZ

KAGAMI! YOU'RE OUT!
ME ?!

...

CHATTER
WHAT'S SEIRIN THINKING?
TAKING HIM OUT?! NO WAY.
IT'S ALL FOR NOTHING IF YOUR COACH SUCKS.
CHATTER
GAB...

I WAS REALLY STARTING TO ...
SHK
BUT... WAIT, WHY ME?

!
COACH NOTICED, YOU SEE.
DON'T WORRY. JUST HIT THE BENCH!
PAT

KAGAMI ...?! DON'T TELL ME...

YEAHHH
YOUR LEG...
IT'S NOT TOTALLY HEALED, RIGHT?
YEAHHH
YEAHH
I'M GOOD... COACH!
I CAN STILL...
HUH ...?!
YEAHHH-SHK
SHK
THE HOSPITAL SAID THERE WAS NO PERMANENT DAMAGE...
...SO IT'S NOT LIKE I'M SAYING YOU CAN'T PLAY AT ALL!
BUT FOR NOW, WE'LL TAPE YOU UP! GET THOSE KICKS OFF!
...
DAMMIT ...! JUST WHEN THINGS WERE GOING WELL...
YEAHH
CHK

YEAHHH...
FWEE
KLANK
RE-BOUND !!
CRAP! I'M SLOWING DOWN...
SH
SHP
RAHHH!!

TOMP TOMP
TO-OH QUICKLY COUNTERS!
YEAHHH
SHOOT... #7 IS 6'3" AND #6 IS 6'4"... WE'RE AT A SERIOUS DISADVANTAGE DOWN LOW WITH KAGAMI OUT OF THE MIX...!!
WE CAN'T GET A RE-BOUND!
YEAHHH
NO MATTER HOW YOU LOOK AT IT...
...THIS IS BAD.
YEAHHH
THE REMAINING FOUR SECOND-YEARS ARE RENDERED USELESS THANKS TO MOMOI'S FORESIGHT.
INDEED, KAGAMI HAS LEFT QUITE A LARGE HOLE IN THIS TEAM...!
YEAHHH
SEIRIN WOULD ORDINARILY USE KUROKO TO RACK UP POINTS, BUT...
YEAHHH

YEAHHH
THE LEAD'S GETTING BIGGER!
TO-OH ACADEMY
5:01
SEIRIN
38
2ND
29
YEAHHH!
YEAHHH
WE'LL ALL...
YEAH, I KNOW...
...TAKE TO-OH DOWN TOGETHER!
RIGHT?
YOU NEED TO TRUST IN THE OTHERS.
RELAX, KAGAMI!
COME ON...
TCH...
HOLD ON FOR JUST A LITTLE MORE...!
THANKS!
NICE!
SHAH
YEAHHH
ALL FINISHED!
YOUR LEGS SHOULDN'T GIVE YOU ANY MORE TROUBLE DURING THIS GAME...
...SO GET OUT THERE!
I'M SORRY...

YEAHHH
SURE, WE WERE GOING ON ABOUT THE WHOLE "TEAM EFFORT" THING...
...BUT THAT'S JUST A STYLE TAUGHT TO ME BY A CERTAIN SOMEONE.
NORMALLY I WOULDN'T PLAY SOMEONE WHO'S NOT 100 PERCENT, BUT...
WE CAN'T WIN WITHOUT YOU, KAGAMI-KUN...
YEAHHH
I'M STILL A LITTLE GREEN AT THIS MYSELF.
I'M NOT PERFECT WHEN IT COMES TO DRAWING OUT EVERYONE'S POTENTIAL...
THAT'S WHY I HAVE TO RELY ON YOU, KAGAMI-KUN, HURT OR NOT...
I HATE HOW POWER-LESS I FEEL...!
YEAHHH
YOU MANAGE OUR TRAINING. YOU SCOUT. YOU CALL PLAYS FROM THE BENCH. YOU MASSAGE US AND TAPE US UP...
IN FACT, I'D SAY YOU DO TOO MUCH.
UM... THAT REALLY YOU?
COACH?
HUH?
THAT WASN'T LIKE YOU AT ALL!
...
YEAHHH

YEAHH
SO STAND TALL AND PROUD!
AT LEAST DURING GAMES.
YEAHHH
HOW PUMPED DO YOU EXPECT ME TO BE IF YOU SEND ME OUT THERE WITH AN APOLOGY?
THINK ABOUT IT.
COACH...
YEAH
BZZZZ
SEIRIN MAKES A SUBSTITUTION!
GET OUT THERE!
SHK
SURE!
YOU'VE SURE GOT A MOUTH ON YOU!
KADUMMY!
YEAHHH

GOOD, GOOD. GET NICE AND PUMPED.

...!!
YOU...
YOU MIGHT JUST MANAGE TO MAKE THIS FUN FOR ME.

YEAHHH
AOMINE !!
SMAK!
YEAHHH
YEAHHH
YOU'RE FINALLY HERE! SHEESH ...
GET YOUR GEAR ON AND GET OUT HERE!!
HUH?
BUT WE'RE ALREADY WINNING ?
NO.
HIT THE COURT!
YEAHHH
YEAHHH
TO-OH ACADEMY
0:51
SEIRIN
48
39
AND THERE'S STILL A WHOLE MINUTE LEFT IN THE SECOND QUARTER ?
GAH! I SHOULD'VE TAKEN MY SWEET TIME GETTING HERE.

UH...
FINE...
SIGH
IN THAT CASE...
WELL...
LET'S DO THIS!

KUROKO'S BASKETBALL TAKE 8 BLOOPERS

46TH QUARTER: NOT BAD AT ALL
SEIRIN
5
4

FWE
WE
E

TO-OH MAKES A SUBSTITUTION.
TO-OH ACADEMY
BZZ
0:31
39
49

RA
W
R...
桐皇
GAKUEN
5
10
5
4
3
2
1

46TH QUARTER:
NOT BAD AT ALL

OHAW
YEAHHH
SEIRI
YEAHHH
5
4
3
2
1

YEAHHH
GULP...
EVERY-ONE CAN...
EVEN WITHOUT COACH'S INSIGHT, I CAN TELL HE'S NO ORDINARY BALLER...
...DAIKI AOMINE!
THAT'S...
YEAHHH
HE'S ONE OF THOSE FIVE PRODIGIES FROM KUROKO'S OLD MIDDLE SCHOOL, WHICH EVERYONE SAYS WAS THE BEST.
EVEN IN AMERICA, I NEVER MET ANYONE THIS GOOD...
YEAHHH
...OF THE MIRACLE GENERA-TION!!
HE'S THE DAMN ACE...
YEAHH

YEAHH
...AND NOW HE'S SHOWED UP, AT THE WORST POSSIBLE TIME...
WE'RE ALREADY TEN POINTS BEHIND...
WE CAN FORGET ABOUT TAKING THE LEAD ON THEM.
YEAHHH
YO, TETSU...
BEEN A WHILE.
I'VE BEEN WONDERING WHAT KIND OF LOOK YOU'D HAVE ON YOUR FACE...
THAT'S A GOOD ONE.
YEAHHH
LOOKS LIKE YOUR HEART'S IN THIS.
YES.
BECAUSE I PROMISED MOMOI-SAN.
YEAHHH
HA HA!
I'VE GOT A GOOD IDEA WHAT YOU WANNA SAY TO ME...
SO GO AHEAD AND SHOW ME...
...ON THE COURT.
YEAHHH

YEAHHH
SAY IT ONCE YOU'VE WON.
YES.
YEAHHH
YEAHHH

YEAHHH
IF YOU THINK YOU CAN.
YEA
WE CAN.
JUST WATCH!
...!
THIS IS...
YEAHHH
BAP
FWEE!
SHK

*AN ISOLATION PLAY IS AN OFFENSIVE STRATEGY THAT GIVES ONE PLAYER SPACE TO WORK WHILE THE REMAINING PLAYERS MOVE AWAY FROM THE BALL.

SH
...TO LET BOTH TEAMS' ACES...
...GO ONE-ON-ONE.
K...
BAP...
SHK!

H!!
SHK
HELP !!
SHK
FAST...! BUT...
THROUGH THE LEGS, INTO A CROSS-OVER...!
HOW'D HE ZOOM PAST KAGAMI SO EASILY?!

WHOOS
SHUP
I NEVER KNEW A HUMAN COULD MOVE THAT FAST!!
WOW ...
SHK
YEAH
OHHHHHH!

SM
ACK
桐皇
GAKU

HUH ?!
HE CAUGHT UP DURING MY SPIN MOVE
...
HE BLOCKED HIM!!
NICE GOING, KAGAMI !!
FROM THAT STANCE INTO A JUMP ...?!
SO HIGH !!
FAST-BREAK!!
SHK
BLOCK!
NOTHING FAST ABOUT YOU SLOW-POKES...
WE'VE BEEN WAITING HERE, TWIDDLING OUR THUMBS!
SHK
SHK
NO! THEIR DEFENSE GOT BACK QUICKLY.
AND THEY'RE STILL READING OUR UPPER-CLASSMEN'S MOVES ...!!

OOM

THAT WAS...
WHA...
SNAG
FW
ONLY KAGAMI COULD CATCH THAT...
GO, KAGAMI!
KURO-KO'S IGNITE PASS !!

SMACK

SINCE KAGAMI PUT HIM OFF-BALANCE, HE WAS BEHIND, BUT STILL...
TOO FAST!

BZZZZZZ
0:00

AH? THOUGHT I MIGHT AS WELL SCORE BEFORE THE BUZZER WENT OFF, BUT...
HUH?
IT'S OVER?

TCH...
WHAT THE HECK WAS THAT...?

THE SECOND QUARTER IS OVER.
UH...
OH...
OHHH... OHHHHHHH !!
RIWRR

YEAHHH
HEY!
NOT BAD AT ALL.
YEAHHH
YEAHHH
...LEMME SHOW YOU JUST HOW GOOD YOU HAD IT.
IF YOU THOUGHT BEING BEHIND ONLY TEN POINTS WAS BAD...
YEAHHH

YEAHHH
AS ALWAYS... HE GETS ON MY NERVES.
AOMINE-CHI...
CHATTER
HE'S CRAZY FAST!!
I'M NO SCOUT, BUT I CAN TELL THAT MUCH AT LEAST.
WHOA...
SO THAT'S AOMINE...
CHATTER...
YEAHHH
HE'S SO SLUG-GISH...
BARELY MOTIVATED AT ALL...
YOU ...!!
WELL SURE, I WASN'T BEING SERIOUS. I'M TIRED.
HA HA...
HUH?
THAT GUY BLOCKED YOUR SHOT LIKE IT WAS NOTHING...
DAMN YOU, AOMINE. PLAY SERIOUSLY FOR ONCE !!
YEAHHH
BUT IN THE SECOND HALF...
...I'M GOING ALL OUT.
FOR REAL.

KUROKO'S BASKETBALL TAKE 2 BLOOPERS

47TH QUARTER: LEAVE IT TO US

CHATTER...
THE SECOND QUARTER IS OVER.
THE THIRD QUARTER...
CHATTER
TO-OH ACADEMY
9:51
49
39
...WILL BEGIN AFTER A TEN-MINUTE BREAK.
GAB...
OOO...
4
YES...
POP
HEY, RYO.
YOU GOT WHAT I ASKED FOR?

LEMON SLICES WITH HONEY

GIVE IT HERE! I NEED A BOOST MORE THAN HE DOES!!
AND YOU, SAKURAI! DON'T PAMPER HIM LIKE THAT!!
YOU AIN'T THE MANAGER!!
FWAP

AOMINE!
WHY'RE YOU EATING...? I MEAN, YOU DIDN'T PLAY LONG ENOUGH TO DESERVE A BREAK-TIME SNACK!!
HUH ?!
OOH. DELISH.
NOM

HEY, DON'T EAT THEM ALL!!
WHAT WAS THAT ?!
I DON'T WANT ANY ANY-MORE.
NONE FOR YOU, FOOL !!
OOH, TASTY !!
CHOMP
CHOMP
TMP TMP
MUNCH MUNCH

AHH...
AWE-SOME.
POP...
DON'T WORRY. I BROUGHT SOME TOO.

DOOM...

NOW, FOR OUR COME-BACK IN THE SECOND HALF...
GOOD WORK IN THE FIRST HALF!
...IT'S TIME FOR AN ENERGY BOOST!!
I'VE GOT LEMONS WITH HONEY!

YOU GOT ANY MORE, SAKURAI ?!
SORRY, ALL OUT...
YEAH. SATSUKI SUCKS AT COOKING.
CAN THIS EVEN BE CONSID-ERED COOKING ?!
HUH ?!
ZING
4

DOOM...

YOU GOT SOME, MITOBE ?!
THIS WAY... THERE'S MORE TO ENJOY.
BUT I WASHED THEM. CAN'T YOU JUST EAT THEM, RIND AND ALL...?
CUT THEM! I ALWAYS SAY, YOU GOTTA CUT THEM FIRST!!
NOD...
TMP...

?
YOU DON'T WANT ANY, KUROKO ?

...
MUNCH
THANK HEAVENS FOR MITOBE.
MUNCH
MUNCH

NO. I'M FINE.

YOU PLAYED EXTENSIVELY IN THE FIRST HALF, KUROKO-KUN, SO I'LL HAVE YOU HANG BACK FOR NOW...
AND YOU'D BETTER REFUEL.
UM...

...

HUH?

FOR THE SECOND HALF...
COULD YOU KEEP ME IN THE WHOLE TIME?

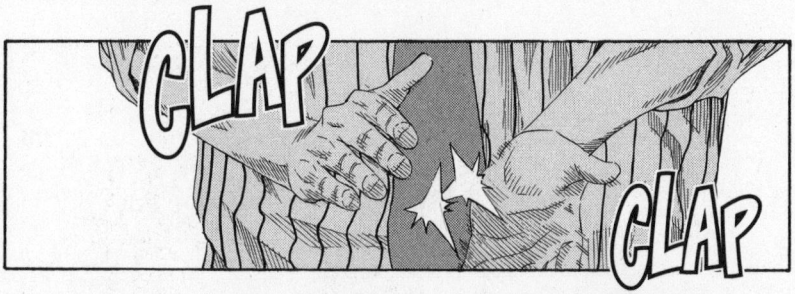
CLAP
CLAP

LET'S TALK SECOND HALF.
HEY NOW, IT'S TOO SOON TO REST ON OUR LAURELS.

4
AOMINE !!
GET BACK HERE !!
HOPEFULLY I CAN GET SOME KIND OF A WORKOUT.

YEAH. GIVE ME THE BALL.

AOMINE-KUN...

AIN'T THAT GOOD ENOUGH ?
THE SECOND HALF IS MINE...
DAMN YOU...

AS LONG AS WE'RE CLEAR ON THIS...
SHOW SOME REAL HUSTLE OUT THERE.

YEAH, YEAH.
KCHAK...

WAKA-MATSU ...
TRY NOT TO ALWAYS GET BENT OUT OF SHAPE.
EVEN YOU, CAP-TAIN ...?

BUT, COACH !!
WELL ...
OBVIOUSLY HE WON'T BE DOING EVERY-THING.
BUT OUR PLAYS WILL CENTER AROUND AOMINE-KUN.
BUT WHAT ABOUT ...?
YOU KEEP CLOSE TO ADMINE-KUN, SAKURAI-SAN.

BUT HIS ATTI-TUDE ...
ISN'T HE GETTING A LITTLE TOO FULL OF HIMSELF ?!
DOES IT REALLY MATTER? LET HIM THINK WHAT HE WANTS.
HUH ?
MIGHT MAKES RIGHT. THAT'S ALL.

SURE, IN A BAD LIGHT, IT'S ARRO-GANCE...
BUT ON THE FLIP SIDE, YOU CAN SEE IT AS OVER-WHELMING SELF-CONFIDENCE FROM A STRING OF WINS.

THINK ABOUT TV INTERVIEWS, WHEN PLAYERS GIVE THEIR THOUGHTS.
PLENTY OF THE BEST ATHLETES GET COCKY ALL THE TIME.

BUT DON'T GET ME WRONG.
I'M NOT A FAN OF AOMINE EITHER. BUT I DON'T HATE HIM.

AS LONG AS HE'S SCORING, HIS PERSONALITY'S IRRELEVANT.

AS LONG AS HE WINS FOR US, HE'S IN THE RIGHT.

I DON'T CARE HOW AOMINE ACTS. I ONLY CARE THAT HE PLAYS FOR US...

...BECAUSE HE GIVES US OUR BEST SHOT AT WINNING.

I'M ALWAYS...

SHIVR

...THINKING...

...ABOUT HOW CALCULATING THIS TEAM IS. WE'RE BOUND BY SELF-INTEREST.

IT'S GOT NOTHING TO DO WITH TRUST. IT'S EVERY MAN FOR HIMSELF.

BUT STILL, FOR SOME REASON...

I DON'T FEEL... LIKE LOSING.

CUZ I READ THEM ALL WRONG.

I'M ACTUALLY SORRY, OKAY?

I CAN'T BELIEVE YOU!
HOW COULD YOU SHOW UP SO LATE?
WHAT'S THE BIG IDEA ?!

YOU'RE FACING TETSU-KUN'S TEAM, HERE!!
SO IN THE SECOND HALF, YOU'D BETTER ...
CRAM IT. I KNOW.

NOW I KINDA WISH I'D SHOWN UP EARLIER.

THE SECOND HALF TOO?
2
SEIRIN HIGH SCHOOL LOCKER ROOM

I CAN DO IT. NO...
I WILL DO IT.

MY EAGLE EYE SHOWED ME THAT IT'S ALREADY LOSING EFFECTIVENESS.
YOU SHOULD REST FOR A WHILE.

I KNOW IT'D BE TOUGH FACING AOMINE WITHOUT KUROKO, BUT...
...CAN HE REALLY DO IT? CAN HE KEEP UP HIS MISDIRECTION FOR THE FULL GAME?
I'M AGAINST IT.

CAN HE REALLY DO IT ...?!
WE APPRECIATE YOUR ENTHUSIASM, BUT STILL ...
BUT, IF KUROKO STAYS OUT THERE, CAN HE REALLY HANG ON TIL THE END...?
...AND NOW THAT THEY'VE GOT AOMINE-KUN, IT'S EVEN MORE OF AN UPHILL BATTLE.
WE DIDN'T HAVE THE LUXURY OF GIVING KUROKO REST IN THE FIRST HALF...
WHAT SHOULD WE DO ...?!
CAN I GET ONE OF THESE, COACH?
?!
SIGH...
BECAUSE NO MATTER WHAT...
...I WANT TO BEAT AOMINE-KUN.

SHOVE
EAT UP AND HANG BACK, DUMMY.
MMF...
SEIRIN

YOU'RE THE ONE WHO SAID HOW BASKETBALL CAN'T BE PLAYED ALONE!
LEAVE IT TO US.

BOTH OPTIONS ARE RISKY, SO THERE'S NO CLEAR ANSWER... MIGHT AS WELL...
...GO ALONG WITH OUR TEAM'S ACE, THEN!
FINE...

KUROKO-KUN WILL REST AT THE START OF THE SECOND HALF!
THE FOURTH QUARTER WILL DECIDE IT ALL!

THAT SAID, IF WE CAN'T MAKE A COMEBACK, IT'S ALL FOR NOTHING.
BE READY TO GET OUT THERE IF THINGS ARE LOOKING HAIRY.
NOD
AND EAT SOME LEMONS.
UH...

OUR BIGGEST THREAT IS AOMINE-KUN...
NATURALLY, THERE'S ONLY ONE HERE WHO CAN KEEP UP WITH HIM.

HYUGA-KUN AND IZUKI-KUN, JUST LIKE IN THE FIRST HALF...
...YOU STAY ON MR. I'M SORRY AND FOUR-EYES.

OUR OPPONENT'S STRONGEST INSIDE THE PAINT.
TSUCHIDA-KUN, YOU'RE IN FOR THE THIRD QUARTER.
YOU AND MITOBE-KUN WILL STAY INSIDE!

KAGAMI-KUN!
IT'S ALL UP TO YOU!
GOT IT!

SHK
SHK
KAGAMI-KUN...
HM?
THAT HEAD OF YOURS COOLED DOWN A BIT?

YEAHH
YES.
LISTEN. I'VE NEVER ACTUALLY SEEN HIM AT HIS BEST. NOT SINCE HE REALLY BLOSSOMED.
WHAT'S MORE, I'M SURE HE'S IMPROVED, JUST AS KISE-KUN AND MIDORIMA-KUN HAVE.
YEAHH

LET'S GO, SEIRIN.
FIGHT !!
YEAHHH!!!

JUST WHAT I WAS HOPING TO HEAR.
HAH!
SO GOING FORWARD, HE REPRESENTS AN UNKNOWN QUANTITY.
PLEASE BE CAREFUL OUT THERE.
YEAHHH...
WE HAD OUR TEAM MEETING, JUST LIKE ALWAYS.
WE WERE JUST LIKE ALWAYS, THAT DAY.
HAHH
HAHH
HAHH
!
WE CAME TOGETHER AS A SINGLE, SOLID TEAM AS WE STARTED THE SECOND HALF...
...JUST LIKE ALWAYS.
CHATTER
CHATTER...

FWOO...
LET'S GET THIS STARTED.
桐
GAKU
5
FLAP...

YEAHHH
YOU CAN TELL HE'S SERIOUS !!
HE'S ALL WORKED UP AND SWEATING ALREADY ...
YEAHHH
HOW-EVER ...
HEY.
YOU GOOD AND PUMPED NOW?
I WANNA SEE YOU STRUGGLE TO THE BITTER END.
IF YOU EVEN CAN.
YEAHHH
LET THE THIRD QUARTER BEGIN.
BZZZZZZ
THIS GAME MARKED A TURNING POINT FOR OUR TEAM.
A TURNING POINT THAT WOULD CHANGE US IN A BIG WAY.

KUROKO'S BASKETBALL TAKE 3 BLOOPERS

YEAHHH
SEIRIN

I DOUBT THEY'LL LAST LONG AT THIS RATE.
NO CHOICE, I SUPPOSE, BUT...
...IN THE FIRST HALF, THEY COULD HARDLY DO WITHOUT HIM, EVEN WITH AOMINE ABSENT...
YEAHHH

HM...
!
THEY'RE RESTING HIM?
IS THAT REALLY THE RIGHT CALL?

AOMINE'LL BE EVEN MORE UNSTOPPABLE WITH KUROKO OUT OF THE GAME...
YOU'RE RIGHT...
YEAHHH

THINKING ABOUT HOW FAST HE'S GROWN, I FEEL LIKE WE MIGHT SEE A MIRACLE.
BUT...
STILL...
YEAHHH

YEAHHH
THAT GUY ...
HE JUST MIGHT PULL IT OFF ...
THEY'RE PLAYING AOMINE!!
YEAHHH
WHOA!
YEAHHH
GAKUEN
48TH QUARTER:
NOTHING BUT LUNATICS
YEAHHH

THIS IS THE MIRACLE GENERATION'S ACE AND SUPER SCORER WE'RE TALKING ABOUT...!!
PLAYING...? WITHOUT A DOUBT, THE WHOLE SECOND HALF WILL BE HIS!
YEAH
...
YEAHHH
COME ON!
FIRST WE'VE GOTTA AT LEAST TRY TO MAKE A DENT.
...WE'LL ALL BE RUNNING ON EMPTY, IN THE FOURTH QUARTER.
IF WE START FLOUNDERING AND KUROKO HAS TO BE PUT IN...
KAGAMI...!
SHK...
BAP
BUT, WELL...
SHK
SOMETHING'S DIFFERENT. NOT LIKE THAT TIME IN THE PARK.
IT LOOKS LIKE THERE'S A FIRE IN HIS EYES.
YEAHH

B
IT'S NO USE!!
AP!

YEAHHH
AGAIN ?!
EVEN KAGAMI CAN'T KEEP UP WITH HIM?!
JUST CAN'T KEEP UP!!
I DIDN'T EVEN GO FOR HIS FAKE...
CRAP!
SHK
FWIP!!
AND THERE'S TWO OF 'EM!!
THAT'S SOME QUICK HELP !!
SEIRIN
9
5
SHK
YEAHH
YEAHHH

5
SEIN
9
FWIP
!!

YEAHHH
STOPPING ON A DIME AND SHIFTING BACK AT THAT SPEED?!
A FADE-AWAY ?!
MY EYES CAN BARELY KEEP UP!
HE'S MAKING MITOBE AND TSUCHIDA LOOK DOWNRIGHT SLOW!!
EACH ONE OF HIS ACTIONS HAPPENS LIGHTNING QUICK...
YEAHHH
FWIP
GAKUEN
5
...AND DECELERATION FROM MAX TO ZERO.
THERE'S ALSO HIS ACCELERATION FROM ZERO TO MAX...
IT'S NOT JUST A MATTER OF HIS TOP SPEED WHEN TAKING ACTION.
YEAHHH
THAT IS TO SAY, HIS AGILITY.
EVEN AMONG *US*, AOMINE WAS ALWAYS ON ANOTHER LEVEL IN THAT SENSE.

SWI
PE

SWISH!
HE'S EVEN FASTER THAN BEFORE!
NOT GOOD ENOUGH ...
DAMN...
THIS GUY...
YEAHHH
ICHI-OH ACADEMY
9:41
SEIRIN
51
3RD
39
OH NO ...!!
EVEN I COULDA PULLED THAT ONE OFF...!
TCH!
SHK
UGH!
YEAHHH
YEAHHH

WHOOSH
SWIP
YEAHHH
A FAST BREAK!
YEAHHH

SLAM IT IN, KAGAMI !!
TAKE THIS !!
GUH

SMACK

BUT ...
IS HE SERIOUS ?
GUESS NOT.

YOU THOUGHT SOME SLOW-POKE MOVES LIKE THAT WOULD CUT IT?
NO, MATTER HOW FAST I GET OUT ON OFFENSE, I CAN'T SHAKE HIM!

GAH!
AGAIN?!

YEAHHH
HIS POSI-TIONING BACK THERE...
RIGHT AT THE FREE THROW LINE.
YEAHH
DID HE THINK HE COULD DUNK FROM THE FREE THROW LINE OR SOMETHING?
SHEESH...
HA HA.
YEAHHH
AHHH, SHOOT!
SO CLOSE.
BUT STILL...
HE'S DOING BETTER THAN I THOUGHT !!
AT THIS RATE, MAYBE...
...
HMPH!
NO GOOD!
YEAHHH

IT REALLY DOESN'T SUIT ME...
GETTING SO SERIOUS ABOUT BASKET-BALL.
SWAY

SOMETHING ABOUT HIM JUST CHANGED!

BAP
I CAN STOP HIM!!
SHK
BUT I'VE GOT HIS SPEED, AND RHYTHM DOWN...
SO NOW...

WHOOPS.
BBAP
?!
SHHK

FW!
OOM
BAP
YEAHHH
STUMBLE
WHAT THE HELL ARE THESE MOVEMENTS?
I CAN'T READ THEM.
IT'S REALLY UNORTHODOX...
YEAHHH
HE'S PLAYING WITH A FLUID...
I SAW THIS ALL THE TIME IN AMERICA...
SKK
IT'S JUST HERKY-JERKY MOVEMENTS WITHOUT A SET FORM...
NO!
GAH?!
YEAHHH

NOT GONNA HAPPEN !!
SEIRIN
10
5
4

TOMP!
THREE OF THEM ?!
WAHHH ?!
SH
UP!
HE STILL GOT PAST THEM ?!
BUT...
HE'S CAUGHT UNDER THE HOOP!!
THEY GOT HIM!!

WI
SH
8
4
5

...HIS PLAYING STYLE!
IT'S LIKE HE'S GOING OUT OF HIS WAY TO MIX UP...
HOW...?!
THIS GUY BREAKS THE MOLD !!
16
SWISH
COMMON SENSE CAN'T ACCOUNT FOR WHAT HE'S DOING!
BAP
ALL YOU MIRACLE GENERATION GUYS ARE...
...NOTHING BUT LUNATICS.

KUROKO'S BASKETBALL BLOOPERS

TAKE 1

49TH QUARTER: LET'S END THIS
GAKUEN
BAP BAP BAP
SHK
YEAH
GUH!
SH
YEAHHH
HE DOESN'T HAVE A SHOT FROM THERE!
HE DIDN'T GET PAST HIM.
HE JUMPED AWAY FROM THE HOOP ?!
SHUP

FINISHING

YEAHHH
WHAT WAS THAT SHOT ?!
A JUMP SHOT...
NO... A HOOK SHOT ?!
YEAHHH
49TH QUARTER:
LET'S END THIS
HOW'D THAT GO IN?!
IT LOOKED LIKE HE WAS JUST FLINGING THE BALL...
I CAN'T READ HIS MOVEMENTS AT ALL!!
WHAT ?!
YEAHHH

...ARE COMPLETELY FORMLESS.

AOMINE'S DRIBBLING AND SHOOTING MOTIONS...

COMPLETE FREEDOM...
THAT'S WHY...
...HE'S AN UNSTOPPABLE SCORER.
THAT IS WHY DAIKI AOMINE IS THE ACE OF THE MIRACLE GENERATION!

YEAHHH...
SHK...
TO-OH ACADEMY
8:11
SEIRIN
55
39
BAP...
HE'S FULL OF OPENINGS.
TOMP
SHK

YEAHH
HE'S JUMPING EVEN HIGHER THAN BEFORE!
SO HIGH !!
SHU
P
ACK!
DAMN! SUCH A WEIRD RHYTHM !!
YEAH
STOP HIM, KAGAMI !!
YEAH. SURE, SURE.
YOU CAN JUMP. WELL DONE.
SHK
BAS-TARD!

BUT THAT TRICK'S GETTING OLD.

SWISH!!
YEAHHH
HE WAS PRACTICALLY HORIZONTAL WHEN HE MADE THE SHOT!
HOW ON EARTH ?!
YEAHHH
...BUT HIS ARE ALL OVER THE PLACE.
NORMALLY, THE BEST SHOOTERS HAVE A CONSISTENT ARC ON THEIR SHOTS...
AND HE STILL DOESN'T MISS!!

YEAHHH
IF HE'S GONNA SCORE REGARDLESS, THEN I'VE JUST GOTTA SCORE MORE.
GRAAAP! THERE'S NO WAY TO TELL WHAT HE'S GONNA DO NEXT!!
YEAHHH
YEAH!
I'VE GOTTA WIN WITH HEIGHT!!
IF HE'S GOT ME BEAT ON SPEED, THEN ...
SEIRIN
SHUP
CAN'T STOP ME IF HE CAN'T REACH!!
BAP

FWIP...
YOU'VE ALREADY LOST IT.
SORRY. TOO SLOW...
?!
SH
K
KAGAMI'S FAST!
WAIT, YOU...
WHOA!
ZOOM!
SHK...

YEAHH
YET...
HE STILL CAN'T CATCH UP?!
NO WAY... BEING QUICK IS ONE THING ...
...BUT HE'S BEATING KAGAMI WHILE DRIB-BLING!
YEAHHH
JUST STOP HIM ALREADY.
AOMINE'S GETTING ALL THE ATTEN-TION!!
HUH ?!
YEAHHH

RAWRRR!
LIKE HELL I'M GIVING UP!!
SLAM
DW...
WOBBLE...
TWEEE

FLIK。。。

..AND HE STILL CAN'T DO ANYTHING!
NO WAY... KAGAMI'S GOING ALL OUT...
THAT'S WHAT WE ALL BELIEVED IN OUR HEARTS...
THERE HAD TO BE A WAY THIS TIME TOO...
...BUT WE WERE FOOLING OURSELVES.
SEIRIN
4
WHEN WE WERE UP AGAINST KISE, AND THEN MIDORIMA...
...HE ALWAYS FOUND A WAY, NO MATTER HOW GOOD THEY WERE...

YEAHHH
SCORE AND ONE!
YEAHHH
FREE THROW !!
SEIRIN
TO-OH ACADEMY
HEY, HEY, IS THAT ALL YOU GOT?
I THOUGHT THIS TIME WOULD BE DIFFER-ENT...
YOUR BASKET-BALL, I MEAN.
...CAN'T BE STOPPED!
AO-MINE...

YEAHHH
THE ONLY ONE WHO CAN BEAT ME IS ME.
YOU JUST CAN'T DO IT ON YOUR OWN.
YEAHHH
GET OUT HERE... TETSU !!
GAKUEN
5
YEAHHH
WE'RE DOWN TWENTY ...
WE'VE JUST GOTTA STAY DETER-MINED ...
HERE I GO.
LET'S DO THIS.
YEAHHH
KUROKO-KUN...
IT'S FINE. I'VE RESTED ENOUGH.
YEAHH

SHOW ME...
SEIRIN
11
SEIRIN

S
SH
...THE POTEN-TIAL...
...OF YOUR SHADOW AND THIS NEW LIGHT.

KUROKO'S BASKETBALL TAKE 9 BLOOPERS

SEIRIN MAKES A SUBSTITUTION.
50TH QUARTER: YOUR BASKETBALL

KURO-KO...

IT'S WAY TOUGHER THAN I THOUGHT, FOR ME ALONE...
I DON'T UNDERSTAND WHAT YOU'RE SAYING.
WHY ARE YOU APOLOGIZING?
HUH ?!

SORRY.
SEIRIN

SHUT UP.
I KNOW THAT!

WE ALWAYS INTENDED TO FIGHT THIS BATTLE AS A TEAM.
IF WINNING WERE THAT SIMPLE, THERE WOULD BE NO CHALLENGE.

50TH QUARTER: YOUR BASKETBALL

YEAHHH
YEAHHH
桐皇
GAKUEN
桐皇
GAKUEN
6
YEAHHH
OOH.
TETSU-KUN...
FWEE
PLEASE!!
KUROKO-CHI...!
LET'S RUMBLE!
YEAHHH

SNAP...
BOOM

HUH ?
SHK
THE SUPER LONG-DISTANCE PASS HE USED AGAINST SHUTOKU!
THAT'S ...
YEAHHH
BUT...
YEAHHH
WHAT A PASS!
I KNEW IT.
OF COURSE YOU'D CATCH UP.
PISSES ME OFF TO DO THIS, BUT...
TOUP
AOMINE'S JUST AS QUICK!!
SHK

FLIK
SHK
MAKE IT COUNT.
CAP-TAIN !!
SHP
WHAT'S UP, KAGAMI? THAT WAS...
...A PRETTY NICE PASS, FOR YOU!
YEA
OHH ?
YEAHHH
YEAHHH

FWISH!
SWISH
SEIRIN
4
TO-OH ACADEMY
5:14
SEIRIN
59
42
RAWR
OUR FIRST POINTS OF THE SECOND HALF!!
...DID IT!!
YEAHHH!
HE...
RAWR
YEAHH
TCH!
BAP
HE'S REALLY NOT BAD...
JUST NOW, I COULD TELL IT'D CONNECT THE SECOND HE SHOT...
YEAHHH
HE'S TOTALLY IN CLUTCH-TIME MODE!!
SHOCK
WHEN I'M SHOOTING, JUST PREPARE TO LAVISH SOME PRAISE!
YOU BETTER NOT'VE BEEN PRAYING, LITTLE FIRST-YEARS!
RRMBBB

SHUP!
桐皇
AKUEN
4
YEAHH
FLIK
SHK
MOMOI PREPARED US FOR THIS...
...BUT IN THE HEAT OF THE ACTION, IT'S EASY TO FORGET HE'S EVEN THERE!
HE'S TOO INVISI-BLE !!
NO!
AM I AN IDIOT ...?
YEAHHH

YEAHHH
YEAHH
TO-OH ACADEMY
6:11
SEIRIN
59
43
SMACK
NICE!
YEAHHH
IT'S A WHOLE NEW GAME WITH KUROKO IN THERE!!
WHOA, TWO IN A ROW!!
YEAHHH
YOU HAVEN'T CHANGED SINCE MIDDLE SCHOOL.
NOT ONE BIT...
SAME AS EVER, TETSU...
...WHEN TETSU'S INVOLVED.
IT REALLY IS DIFFERENT.
YEAHHH

YEAHHH
HOW...
...DIS-APPOINT-ING.
YEAHHH
...!
YEAHH
YEAHHH
RAWR
YES, I DO.
THIS IS MY BASKET-BALL.
YOU STILL THINK YOU CAN WIN LIKE THAT?
AGAINST ME?
YEAHHH

SORRY, BUT I KNOW ALL ABOUT YOUR PASSES, TETSU.
YOUR MIS-DIRECTION CRAP TOO.
GAKUEN
OR DIDJA FORGET WHO WAS ON THE RECEIVING END OF THOSE PASSES ALL THOSE YEARS?
IGNITE PASS !!
KA
TOMP
FOOM
SHK...
...!
LET'S KEEP THIS MOMENTUM GOING!
GO!

YOUR PASSES...
PII

SH
...WON'T WORK HERE.

EVEN TAKAO-KUN COULDN'T STOP OUR ACE IN THE HOLE!
HOW ...?!
WHA-?!
SHK
BAP
TCH!
BAP BAP
WHOOSH
SHK

FWOOM!
HOW'S ONE GUY THIS GOOD?
HE GOT PAST THREE OF THEM?!
SHK
TAP
BAP
SHK
SHK
SHUP
NICE, THEY MADE IT BACK!!
KAGAMI, KUROKO! STOP HIM !!

GAK
5

?!
THUD THUD...
HE GOT PAST... ALL FIVE ?!
NO WAY...
HOW SAD... YOU'RE STILL THE SAME AS YOU WERE AT THE MIDDLE SCHOOL NATIONALS FINAL.
AND BY "SAME," I MEAN YOU HAVEN'T GROWN AT ALL.
IN THE END, I GUESS AKASHI WAS RIGHT...

YOUR BASKET-BALL...
桐皇
GAKUEN
5

...JUST ISN'T ENOUGH.

KUROKO'S BASKETBALL BLOOPERS

TAKE 1

51ST QUARTER:
ONE THING I WON'T DO!!
SHK
LET THE FOURTH QUARTER BEGIN.
SHK
WHAT A LEAD...
...
TO-OH ACADEMY
9:56
4TH
SEIRIN
82
51
FLI
K!
ZOOM!!

SMACK!!
WHOOSH
BAP
SHK

HO
WHA—?!
SHOOTING WHILE SPINNING?!
HE'S GETTING CRAZIER AND CRAZIER!
SWISH
OSH
YEAHHH
KRIK
YEAHHH

WHY?! HE SHOULD'VE RECOVERED BY NOW, AND I TAPED HIM UP ON TOP OF THAT...
HOW'S HE STILL GETTING WORSE?
IS IT HIS LEG ?!
KAGAMI-KUN'S LOOKING A LITTLE...
YEAHHH
NO! THIS IS...
...!!
JUST TAKE A SEAT.
THERE'S NO PROBLEM WITH MY TAPING.
AGAIN? WHY...?!
COACH.
HUH ?
SEIRIN MAKES A SUBSTI-TUTION.
KAGAMI !!
YEAHHH
I'M FINE, I SWEAR.
AND THE GAME... NOW, MORE THAN EVER, I...
YEAHHH

YEAHHH
I SAID TAKE A SEAT!!
YEAH
YEAHHH
GRR...
HE'S BEEN SUBCONSCIOUSLY COMPENSATING FOR HIS HURT LEG THIS WHOLE TIME.
BUT THAT MEANS HIS OTHER LEG IS OVERBURDENED...
I KNEW IT.
...
YEAHHH

...FOR THE REMAINING TWO DAYS OF THE FINALS LEAGUE, HE'S OUT.
AND TO TOP IT OFF...
I CAN'T PUT HIM BACK OUT THERE...
YEAHHH
YEAH
YEAHHH
THERE'S NO NEED...
I THINK.
WELL, DID YOU?
I...
MOMOI-SAN, YOU DID HAVE A COUNTER-STRATEGY FOR HIM, RIGHT?
FINALLY, IT'S COMING TO A HEAD.
YEAHHH

YEAHHH
YEAHHH
WHOA...
THAT GUY'S SOME-THING ELSE.
YEAHHH
YEAHHH
HUH ?!
LOOKS ABOUT READY TO KILL SOME-ONE.
GAKUEN
BUT THIS GUY, EVEN AFTER THIS BEATING ...
HELL, EVEN MORE THAN BEFORE ...
HONEST-LY, EVEN I...
...MIGHT END UP THAT WAY IF I HAD TO FACE HIM.
HE STRIPS AWAY THEIR WILL TO EVEN TRY.
...IS OVER-WHELMED, AND SOME EVEN QUIT, AFTER REALIZING THE DIFFERENCE IN SKILLS.
EVERYONE WHO GOES UP AGAINST AOMINE...
YEAHHH

HE'S BURNING UP, OVER THERE...
WITH RAGE.
YEAHHH
FAR FROM THROWING IN THE TOWEL, HE'S READY FOR REVENGE.
NEVER SEEN A GUY LIKE THAT BEFORE.
YEAHH
YEAHHH

YEAHHH
BUT I WAS FORCED TO SHOOT ...
IT'S OFF ...!!
OUR DEFENSE CAN'T STOP AOMINE, AND MOMOI'S ANTICIPATING OUR OFFENSIVE MOVES...
SHUP
YEAHHH
KLANK
YEAHHH
YEAHHH

HAHH
HAHH
YEAHHH
YEAHHH
YEAH
I CAN HARDLY BEAR TO WATCH.
EVEN MORE THAN BEFORE, IT'S TOO ONE-SIDED.
IT'S ALL OVER, RIGHT?
WE CAN'T GET AHEAD HERE.
SHOULD WE JUST SWITCH HIM OUT FOR KOGA?
KUROKO'S LONG SINCE REACHED HIS LIMIT.
YEAHHH
TO-OH ACADEMY
SEIRIN
A FORTY-POINT LEAD...
NOTHING LEFT FOR THEM BUT TO STRUGGLE...
YEAHHH

BA
P
IT'S OVER FOR YOU.
THAT DIDN'T TAKE LONG AT ALL.
YEAHHH
YEAHHH
YOU'RE WORSE THAN A RUN-OF-THE-MILL PLAYER AT THIS POINT.
AND THAT MIS-DIRECTION? FINISHED.
YOU'RE BARELY STILL STANDING.
YOUR LIGHT'S GONE.
THOSE PASSES YOU'RE SO PROUD OF WON'T WORK.
TETSU.
THIS IS MY WIN.
YEAHHH
EVEN IF YOU THINK THIS IS ALL MEANING-LESS...
...I CAN'T TURN MY BACK ON ANY CHANCE.
UNTIL OUR CHANCES DROP TO ZERO, I WON'T GIVE UP.
THERE'RE NO MIRACLE COMEBACKS IN THIS GAME. YOU DON'T HAVE A SHOT IN HELL...
IT'S NOT...
...OVER YET.
YEAHHH
YEAH

THAT'S WHY GIVING UP IS THE ONE THING...

...I WON'T DO!
SEIRIN
9

YEAHHH
YEAHHH
I CLEARLY CAN'T SUB HIM OUT AFTER THAT.
SHEESH...
...BY SOME LITTLE FIRST-YEAR'S BURNING SPIRIT.
WE CAN'T LET OURSELVES BE SHOWN UP...
...
SHP!!
MAKE SOME NOISE! TO THE VERY END!
DON'T HOLD A FUNERAL FOR US JUST YET, BENCH!
YEAHHH
YEAHHH

YEAHHH
OUR BOYS OUT THERE HAVEN'T GIVEN UP YET...
...SO HOW CAN WE SIT HERE SO QUIETLY?
YEAHHH
RIGHT...
OF COURSE.
DE-FENSE!
DE-FENSE!
DE-FENSE!
LET'S CUT INTO THEIR LEAD, BIT BY BIT. KEEP GOING 'TIL IT'S OVER.
YEAHH
I GUESS...
...I'LL GIVE YOU THAT MUCH.
DE-FENSE!
YEAHHH

YOU SUCK AT GIVING UP.

NOT ONE OF US GAVE UP.
EVERY-ONE FOUGHT TO THE BITTER END.
EVEN SO, THE GAP CONTIN-UED TO WIDEN.
NEXT TIME...
WE'LL WIN... NEXT TIME!
NO ONE SHED A TEAR.

THAT DAY, WE EXPERIENCED AN UTTERLY CRUSHING...

...DE-
FEAT.
TO-OH
ACADEMY
0:0
SEIRIN
112
4TH
55

NOTHING.

YEAHHHHHHHHH
LET'S GO, KUROKO.
TIME TO LINE UP.
RIGHT.

TO-OH ACADEMY WINS!!
TO-OH ACADEMY
0-0
SEIRIN
112
55
WITH A SCORE OF 112 TO 55...

LINE UP!!
THANK YOU FOR THE GAME !!

DOUBLED THEIR SCORE?
WHA–?!

STILL, I'M NOT SURE WHO AMONG US COULD ACTUALLY STOP AOMINE...
THE MIRACLE GENERATION'S ACE IS NO JOKE.

KAGAMI WAS JUST ABOUT THE PERFECT FOIL FOR MIDORIMA.
IT'S NOT QUITE AS SIMPLE AS THAT.

SHUT UP, IDIOT!
IF SEIRIN GOT WHOOPED THIS BAD, IMAGINE THE BEATING WE'D TAKE...
TO-OH IS FREAKING NUTS!
OUCH!

AREN'T YOU A LITTLE BIT SHOCKED?
AT THESE RESULTS, I MEAN?

NOT SURE WHY YOU'RE WORRYING ABOUT ME.
KUROKO IS THE ONE WHO COULD USE SOME SYMPATHY AT THIS POINT.

I CAN HARDLY BELIEVE I WATCHED THIS MATCH UNTIL THE VERY END.
SO SUDDEN!
LATER, KISE.

THE SCORE ASIDE... KUROKO'S STYLE DIDN'T WORK ON AOMINE AT ALL.
THIS MUST HAVE DESTROYED HIM PSYCHO-LOGICALLY.
HUH?

THEY WON'T BE COMING BACK FROM A DEFEAT LIKE THIS OVERNIGHT.
AND SEIRIN IS STILL A YOUNG TEAM.

THEY CAN ONLY HOPE THAT THIS DOESN'T AFFECT THEIR PERFORMANCE IN THE NEXT TWO GAMES.

ALL RIGHT! FIRST MATCH OF THE FINALS LEAGUE...
CRUSHED IT!!
RAWR

WE KNOW. NO NEED TO SHOUT.

...

HE SHOULDA GIVEN UP QUICK.

ESPECIALLY THAT #11. BUT IN THE END, HE WAS JUST TRASH.
WITH HIM GETTING ALL WORKED UP THERE, I WAS SURE THEY'D SUB HIM OUT.
HA HA HA
DIDN'T KNOW WHAT TO THINK OF THESE GUYS AFTER THEY BEAT SHUTOKU.

HEY, NOW. HURRY UP AND GET PACKING.
WE'LL REVIEW AT ANOTHER TIME.

GUH ?!
YOU SURE YAP A LOT FOR A BENCH-WARMER.
IT'S HURTING MY EARS, SO PIPE DOWN.
GEHH ...
WHAT'RE YOU DOING, AOMINE? PUT HIM DOWN!
GAH! WHAT THE HELL?
OMINE-KUN ...

SLA
M

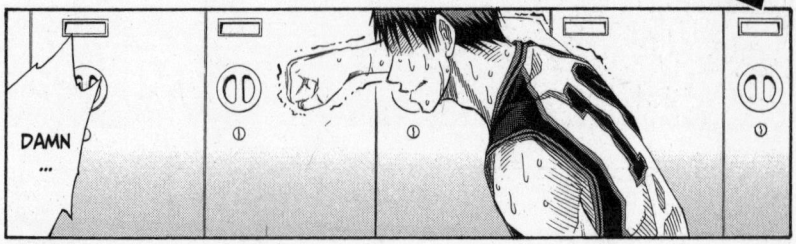
DAMN ...

WE KNEW THAT...
...BUT, THE TRUTH STARTS TO SET IN ONCE THE MATCH ENDS ...

...SO THERE'S NO TIME TO BE IN A FUNK!!
THAT'S RIGHT! THERE'RE STILL TWO MORE GAMES...

WE CAN STILL MAKE IT!
DON'T FLIP OUT, KAGAMI.

THIS WAS WAY TOO MUCH FOR US...

WE'LL TALK ABOUT IT LATER! HEAD HOME FOR NOW!
AND YOU'D BETTER GET YOURSELF TO A DOCTOR, KAGAMI-KUN!
GOT IT.

I REALLY THOUGHT WE COULD DO MORE.
BUT LOOK HOW IT TURNED OUT.

HEY...
THIS MIGHT BE OUR LIMIT.

THE OTHERS ALREADY SPLIT.
LET'S GO, KUROKO.
OKAY...

UP AGAINST A POWER-HOUSE LIKE THAT...
EVEN US TEAMING UP...
...WASN'T ENOUGH TO WIN.
SEIRIN

SEIRIN
I PROMISE.
I'LL BEAT AOMINE-KUN.
THE ONLY ONE WHO CAN BEAT ME...
...IS ME.
SAY IT ONCE YOU'VE WON.
LET'S BEAT HIM GOOD ...
BUMP...
...AND SHOW HIM WHAT A MORON HE IS.

SLAM

TWO DAYS LATER ...
KAIJO PRIVATE HIGH SC
SWISH

WHAT'RE YOU DOING HERE?
I THOUGHT YOU WENT OFF TO SEE THE LAST GAME OF THE FINALS LEAGUE.
I DID.
BUT NEVER MIND THAT, SENPAI.

HUH? SENPAI?
HUH?
BAP

HOW ABOUT...
...A ONE-ON-ONE?

NO THANKS. WHAT'S THE BIG IDEA?
I JUST GOT THE SUDDEN URGE TO PLAY SOME BALL.
JUST TELL ME HOW THE GAME ENDED.

HUH?

KRAK
NO WAY! AND I ASKED YOU A QUESTION !!
YOU CAN HAVE THE BALL FIRST, SENPAI!
OUCH!

SHK!

NOT TO MENTION KUROKO'S SUDDEN DOWN-TURN.

HIS PASSES THAT HAD SAVED OUR BUTTS WHO KNOWS HOW MANY TIMES LOST THEIR EFFECTIVE-NESS. HE WAS A SHADOW OF HIS FORMER SELF.

KAGAMI-KUN HAD TO SIT OUT, WHICH MESSED UP THE TEAM'S CHEMISTRY.

BUT THE SCARS FROM OUR BATTLE AGAINST TO-OH RAN DEEP.

WE GAVE ALL WE HAD IN THE NEXT TWO GAMES.

WE LOST BY A HAIR.

OUR SECOND GAME WAS AGAINST MEISEI HIGH.

IN THIS SORRY STATE, WE FOUGHT TO THE VERY END.

BUT NOT EVERY CHALLENGER CAN BE A WINNER.

	SEIRIN	TO-OH ACADEMY	MEISEI	SE SHI
SEIRIN		● (55–112)	● (78–79)	
TO-OH DEMY	○ (112–55)		○ (150–47)	(1
ISEI	○ (79–78)	● (47–150)		(9
EN-NKAN		● (91–105)	○ (103–54)	

THE THIRD DAY SAW TO-OH ACADEMY'S THIRD WIN, AND IF SEIRIN COULD'VE PULLED OFF A WIN, THAT WOULD'VE MEANT THREE TEAMS WITH ONE WIN AND TWO LOSSES, GIVING US ONE LAST SHOT AT INTER-HIGH.

WE BET IT ALL ON THAT FINAL GAME.

*IN THAT CASE, THE WINNERS WOULD BE DECIDED BY OVERALL POINTS SCORED.

SEIRIN
78
WE LOST.
AND WITH THAT...
4

SENSHINKAN
96
4
...SEIRIN HIGH SCHOOL'S HOPES OF REACHING INTER-HIGH WERE CRUSHED.

YEAHH...
HOW-EVER ...

THAT WASN'T REALLY THE END OF EVERY-THING.
BZZZ BZZZ
BZZZ
BECAUSE AFTER EVERY ENDING...
FLIP...
...COMES A NEW BEGIN-NING.
15:21
Received Text
15:21
Riko Aida
Sorry
We lost.
IN OTHER WORDS ...

52ND QUARTER:
TO A NEW CHALLENGE

TO BE CONTINUED

HIKARU no
Story by YUMI HOTTA
Art by TAKESHI OBATA
The breakthrough series by Takeshi Obata, the artist of Death Note!
Hikaru Shindo is like any sixth-grader in Japan: a pretty normal schoolboy with a penchant for antics. One day, he finds an old bloodstained Go board in his grandfather's attic. Trapped inside the Go board is Fujiwara-no-Sai, the ghost of an ancient Go master. In one fateful moment, Sai becomes a part of Hikaru's consciousness and together, through thick and thin, they make an unstoppable Go-playing team.
Will they be able to defeat Go players who have dedicated their lives to the game? And will Sai achieve the "Divine Move" so he'll finally be able to rest in peace? Find out in this Shonen Jump classic!
RATED A
ALL AGES
ratings.viz.com
SHONEN JUMP
www.shonenjump.com
viz media
www.viz.com
HIKARU-NO GO © 1998 by Yumi Hotta, Takeshi Obata/SHUEISHA Inc.

EYESHIELD 21

STORY BY RIICHIRO INAGAKI
ART BY YUSUKE MURATA

From the artist of *One-Punch Man!*

Wimpy Sena Kobayakawa has been running away from bullies all his life. But when the football gear comes on, things change—Sena's speed and uncanny ability to elude big bullies just might give him what it takes to become a great high school football hero! Catch all the bone-crushing action and slapstick comedy of Japan's hottest football manga!

www.viz.com

www.shonenjump.com

ratings.viz.com

EYESHIELD 21 © 2002 by Riichiro Inagaki, Yusuke Murata/SHUEISHA Inc.

From the creator of ***YuYu Hakusho!***

Hunters are a special breed, dedicated to tracking down treasures, magical beasts, and even other people. But such pursuits require a license, and less than one in a hundred thousand can pass the grueling qualification exam. Those who do pass gain access to restricted areas, amazing stores of information, and the right to call themselves **Hunters**.

HUNTER ハンター × ハンター HUNTER

Story and Art by **YOSHIHIRO TOGASHI**

viz media
www.viz.com

SHONEN JUMP ADVANCED

HUNTERxHUNTER © POT (Yoshihiro Togashi) 1998, 2000

Love triangle!
Comedic antics!!
Gang warfare?!

A laugh-out-loud story that features a fake love relationship between two heirs of rival gangs!

Story and Art by
NAOSHI KOMI

NISEKOI
False Love

It's hate at first sight...rather, a knee to the head at first sight when **RAKU ICHIJO** meets **CHITOGE KIRISAKI**! Unfortunately, Raku's gangster father arranges a false love match with their rival's daughter, who just so happens to be Chitoge! Raku's searching for his childhood sweetheart from ten years ago, however, with a pendant around his neck as a memento, but he can't even remember her name or face!

AVAILABLE NOW!

NISEKOI © 2011 by Naoshi Komi/SHUEISHA Inc.

SHONEN JUMP
WWW.SHONENJUMP.COM

RATED T FOR TEEN
ratings.viz.com

viz media
www.viz.com

MY HERO ACADEMIA

IZUKU MIDORIYA WANTS TO BE A HERO MORE THAN ANYTHING, BUT HE HASN'T GOT AN OUNCE OF POWER IN HIM. WITH NO CHANCE OF GETTING INTO THE U.A. HIGH SCHOOL FOR HEROES, HIS LIFE IS LOOKING LIKE A DEAD END. THEN AN ENCOUNTER WITH ALL MIGHT, THE GREATEST HERO OF ALL, GIVES HIM A CHANCE TO CHANGE HIS DESTINY...

viz media
www.viz.com

BOKU NO HERO ACADEMIA © 2014 by Kohei Horikoshi/SHUEISHA Inc.